More Reversible Quilts

11 New Projects

Sharon Pederson

Martingale®
& COMPANY

CREDITS

CEO • Daniel J. Martin

President • Nancy J. Martin

Publisher • Jane Hamada

Editorial Director • Mary V. Green

Managing Editor • Tina Cook

Technical Editor • Ellen Pahl

Copy Editor • Liz McGehee

Design Director • Stan Green

Illustrator • Laurel Strand

Cover and Text Designer • Shelly Garrison

Photographer • Brent Kane

That Patchwork Place® is an imprint of Martingale & Company®.

More Reversible Quilts: 11 New Projects © 2004 by Sharon Pederson

Martingale & Company
20205 144th Avenue NE
Woodinville, WA 98072-8478 USA
www.martingale-pub.com

Printed in China
09 08 07 06 05 04   8 7 6 5 4 3 2 1

**Library of Congress
Cataloging-in-Publication Data**

Pederson, Sharon.
  More reversible quilts: 11 new projects/Sharon Pederson.
    p. cm.
  ISBN 1-56477-556-9
1. Patchwork—Patterns. 2. Quilting—Patterns.
I. Title.
  TT835.P352 2004
  746.46'041—dc22

                    2004012863

MISSION STATEMENT

Dedicated to providing quality products
and service to inspire creativity.

DEDICATION

To Ann Riviere, Mae Findlay, and Dorothy Nylin—my mother-in-law, my mother, and my friend—role models all.

ACKNOWLEDGMENTS

The list of people to thank has to begin with my husband. He has recently retired (I am, as one friend put it, at the "half-double" part of my life—half the money, double the husband), and instead of having a partner to do things with, he found the door to the studio closed and the computer off-limits. He is even learning to cook.

The second person on the list is Ionne McCauley. I hired her to help me and never has an employer been so blessed. She is a delight to work with, is endlessly creative, and has a killer sense of humor—not to mention a black belt in karate. Her involvement went way beyond helping make the quilts; she kept me sane throughout the process.

As always, my students and friends have shared their innovations and their quilts, notably Mary Ellen Kranz, Sharron Evans, LaVerne Somerville, Jean Biddick, Denise Allen, and Joanne Corfield. Thank you all.

And finally, to the miracle workers at Martingale & Company, a huge thank you again for taking my box full of quilts, my manuscript, and my squiggly drawings and turning them into a wonderful book. With a team that includes Mary Green, Tina Cook, Ellen Pahl, Liz McGehee, Stan Green, Laurel Strand, Shelly Garrison, Brent Kane, Karen Soltys, Donna Lever, Shelley Santa, and Rhoda Reynolds, how could it be anything but successful!

Contents

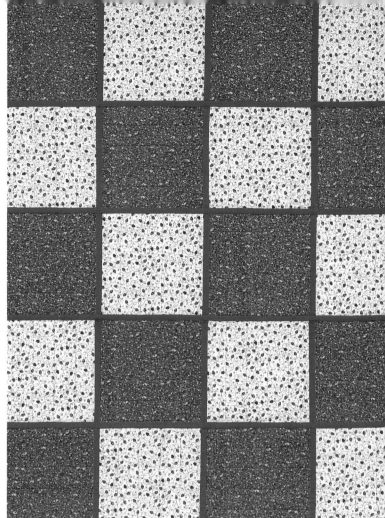

PREFACE

When I was writing *Reversible Quilts*, I realized I would never get all of the variations into one book. Almost as soon as I sent off the manuscript, I started thinking about what to do with the "leftover" projects. Then, as I continued to teach my Reversible Quilts class all over North America and the United Kingdom, my students came up with even more ways to use the technique, so I knew that Book Number Two (or BNT as it affectionately became known) was almost a certainty. To clinch the deal, *Reversible Quilts* was so well received that it went into four printings in its first year alone. It has even been translated into French! It's my hope that *More Reversible Quilts* will enjoy the same degree of popularity.

The years since *Reversible Quilts* was published have been incredibly busy and very exciting. The book opened doors for me and helped gather invitations to teach in some wonderful places. I have made some great new friends and have enjoyed the warm welcome that is offered by quilters everywhere. If I had known how much fun I was going to have, I'd have written the first book much sooner!

One thing I know for sure: there are never enough new fabrics, and there are never enough new books (with lots of colored pictures) to satisfy the typical quilter. We have a craving for beauty that can only be satisfied by one more yard of delicious fabric or the latest book. I once overheard a conversation between a husband and wife in a quilt shop when she announced she was buying my book. He said, "Why do you need another book about quilting, you already have one?" The other customers almost rolled on the floor. The poor man gave us his best imitation of a smile and retreated to the car. I don't have to tell you: she bought the book.

So, quilters, here it is—another book I hope you will find irresistible. Not only that, I hope you find it a useful tool in your collection of must-have books.

Small Quilts?

One final note before we get right into it. Recently, some airlines changed the allowable weight per bag from 70 pounds to 50 pounds. This effectively eliminates 40 pounds of weight that you are allowed to carry on a plane. What this has meant to quilt teachers is that we either have to make smaller quilts or bring fewer samples to show students when we teach. I opted for smaller quilts. This doesn't mean that reversible quilts all have to be small; it just means that the ones I carry with me (and show in this book) are small.

INTRODUCTION

It's always a good idea to get an overview of a technique before starting a project. Be sure to review the sections describing the basic construction of reversible blocks and how they are joined together. Then take a look at the section on settings and sashing, followed by the section on binding. Armed with all of that technical information, you can proceed with any of the projects in this book or you can let your imagination run free and create your own version of a reversible quilt.

Remember, the right way to make a quilt is the way that works for you. If there is something you don't like about my method, by all means change it to suit yourself. And if you come up with a neat new way to do something, I'd love to hear about it. I have learned so much from my students that I almost feel guilty receiving royalties for this book! (You'll notice I said "almost!")

What has changed since *Reversible Quilts* was published? Well, I've changed the dimensions of the wide side of reversible bindings from 1⅝" to 1¾". This makes the cutting easier to remember. Only a brain surgeon—or a quilter—would worry about a ⅛" difference. Also, I've included the option of drawing a line on the batting to help line up the first two strips. But the biggest change has been the discovery of Hobbs Fusible Batting. I can't believe how much easier it is to work with reversible blocks when you have a bit of fusible "holding on" for you. Unlike fusible web that is permanent once you apply it with heat, Hobbs Fusible Batting can be repositioned if you change your mind. Also, the "glue" washes out the first time you launder your quilt, so it's not permanent.

FABRIC, TOOLS, AND SUPPLIES

You can't make a quilt without fabric. So you have my permission to go out and buy some! You'll also need a sewing machine, rotary cutter, cutting mat, a variety of rulers, thread, needles, scissors, and on and on. Your sewing life will be much happier if you have the right tools and materials. Invest in good quality. The payoff will be beautiful quilts that last for generations.

FABRIC

I am a firm believer in the theory that you can never have too much fabric. I mainly buy one-yard pieces, always 100% cotton, and from whatever independent quilt shop I am nearest to. I buy larger pieces only if I know in advance what I'm going to do with it (a novel concept) or if it is so drop-dead beautiful I know I'll regret not having more than one yard.

Remember, you are going to put a lot of work (and love) into a quilt, and you want it to last a long time, so buy only good-quality materials. I recommend that you shop at an independent quilt shop. To stay in business, they must provide good service and good materials. It is in their best interest to keep you happy, so you can trust them to make sure you are getting value for your money. You will also get lots of help with color choices, suggestions about what you might do to create the look you want, and lots of oohs and aahs when you bring the finished product in to show them—all good reasons to support them.

SEWING MACHINE

Your sewing machine is your friend. Keep it clean and oiled and have it serviced at least once a year. My current machine cost more than my first five cars combined, and I am careful not to neglect its checkups. But even if it were a golden oldie, I'd still pay attention to the service record. There's nothing more frustrating than trying to do something with your machine and having it cough and splutter and refuse to sew. (Well, OK, trying to program the VCR is more frustrating!)

While we're on the subject of sewing machines, you do deserve the best. Whenever you feel you can't justify the expense, just look in the basement or garage and count up the number of tools there for "you-know-who." Then go out and get that machine you've had your eye on. We are taking raw materials and adding value to them with our machines; a good machine is an investment.

WALKING FOOT

This is essential. If your machine does not have a built-in walking foot, you must buy one. (Reread the above paragraph; you deserve the best.) You will be machine quilting without basting, so to prevent puckers and pleats, always use a walking foot.

ROTARY CUTTER AND MAT

I would love to give a "Person of the Year" award to whoever invented the rotary cutter. Whenever I have to cut fabric, I heap blessings on that unknown inventor. You can make a much more accurate cut with a rotary cutter than with scissors, and it's not as hard on your hands. With your rotary cutter, you will need a self-healing mat to protect both your tabletop and the cutter blade. My feelings about both are to buy the biggest ones you can afford and have space for. Be sure to store cutting mats flat and away from any heat source or they will warp. That includes not leaving them in a closed car on a hot day. Ask me how I know that.

Waste Not

From what was left of my ruined cutting mat, I cut out a circle using my kitchen shears and glued it to a turntable I bought at a garage sale. It has been the handiest thing for cutting small pieces, particularly circles. Rather than repositioning the pieces so I am always cutting away from myself, I just turn the table. But don't think you have to cut up one of your mats; now you can purchase ready-made revolving mats in quilt shops and through mail-order catalogs.

RULERS

Along with the rotary cutter and mat, you will need rulers. You'll notice I used a plural there. I have more than 20 rulers, but I'm not suggesting you need that many. I think there are three essential sizes. I started with a 6" x 12" Omnigrid and it's still my favorite. Next is a 12½" square, which is invaluable when making reversible quilts. To round out the trio, I suggest a ruler that is 24" long. It doesn't have to be very wide; 3" is fine. You can do just about anything with this combination.

SEWING-MACHINE NEEDLES AND THREAD

When selecting needles and threads, remember to buy only good-quality products. You will be investing a lot of time in your project and you want it to last. Why risk damaging your quilt with cheap needles or having it weakened by poor-quality thread?

Sewing-Machine Needles: Mystery and confusion seem to reign when it comes to machine needles. In every class, students ask, "What size needle should I use for this project?" And my response is, "What size thread are you using?"

There is a direct relationship between the thread size you are using and the needle. Sewing-machine needles have a groove down the front, which carries the thread as it goes through the fabric and into the bobbin. The thread should fit into that groove. If the groove is too large and there is room for the thread to flutter as it passes back and forth through the needle, the thread may break. The needle makes a hole in the fabric and the thread should fill that hole. If the hole isn't large enough for the thread to fit through, the seam may pucker. Therefore, it is extremely important to use the appropriate-size needle for each thread.

It is recommended that you change your needle after eight hours of sewing. That's right, eight hours. I had one student ask, "You mean, you can change the needle?" I was afraid to ask her how old her machine was.

Thread: Many years ago, I received the following advice about thread.

◆ Match the fiber content of your thread to the fiber content of your fabric.

◆ Use the finest thread and the smallest needle that will do the job.

◆ Never use a thread that is stronger than the fiber of your fabric.

For basic hand and machine sewing, you need a medium-weight 100% cotton thread. To find the weight of the thread, look at the spool and you'll see numbers like 50/3, 60/2, etc. The first number indicates the weight of the thread; the smaller the number, the thicker the thread. The second number indicates how many plies there are; the higher the number, the stronger the thread. That means that 50/3 is thicker and stronger than 60/2. I use 50/3 for all my basic hand and machine sewing.

My favorite color for sewing thread is medium gray. One of my first quilting teachers told me that if you use a thread that is lighter than your fabric, it will look like a picket fence across your quilt, whereas a darker thread will just look like a shadow.

Threading the Needle

To help see the tiny hole in the needle when threading, keep a little plastic fastener (the thing that holds the bread bag closed) by your machine. (I hook mine over the knee lift on my machine.) If you hold it behind the needle, it is much easier to see the eye.

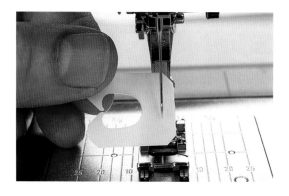

Easy Thread Removal

When you make a mistake (that hardly ever happens, I know, but just in case) and you have clipped all the stitches and pulled the thread out, you are left with lots of annoying little pieces of thread. If you don't pick them off, you can count on them getting caught in the next row of stitching, and then they will be even harder to get out. I keep masking tape near the machine, and when I have to remove all those little threads, I rub the area with masking tape and most of them stick to the tape.

Make a Thread Chart

To make it easier to remember which threads are appropriate for each needle, I made a helpful little chart. I bought four spools of cotton thread in the sizes I use most often (60/2, 50/3, 40/3, 30/3) and one spool of invisible nylon thread (size .004). I typed needle sizes at the top of the chart and thread sizes at the bottom. I cut a piece of thread from each spool and taped it to the appropriate spot on the chart, so now I know which size needle fits each of the five weights of thread.

This chart is also helpful when I want to switch to another fiber, such as metallic or rayon thread, where size numbers do not correspond to cotton sizes. All I do is compare the size of the metallic or rayon thread to the size of the cotton threads on the chart, and I know what size needle to use.

The chart is only a starting point. For every project, particularly if I'm using a new thread, I test it on a piece of the same fabric as my project. If an 80/12 needle is too small for the thread, even though it looked right on the chart, I go up one needle size to see if I get better results.

Needles				
60/8	70/10	80/12	90/14	100/16
60/2	INV	50/3	40/1	30/3
Thread				

BATTING

I'm particularly fond of Hobbs batting. I have been using their Heirloom Cotton (80% cotton and 20% polyester) in most of my quilts for years. It must be quilted every 4", which is not a problem because I like to heavily quilt most things. However, I occasionally make a quilt that I refer to as "my least-favorite nephew" type quilt. These are the nephews who need a little more time to appreciate quilts. You probably have one; he's only 18 years old, so you know he's going to use a quilt to dry the dog or put it in the back of his truck to protect it from being scratched. But you've made a quilt for all the other nieces and nephews, so it's important to make him one, too. My advice in this situation is use dark colors, choose a pattern that has very large pieces, and do minimal quilting. Choose Hobbs Organic with Scrim and you can leave big chunks of it unquilted.

Recently, Hobbs came out with a fusible batting, and I just love it. I have used it extensively in my reversible quilts, and it is so much easier than having to pin. The fusible batting pretty much eliminates the slippage you get when sewing through a quilt sandwich. If you hold the iron about $\frac{1}{8}$" above the surface of the quilt and push the button that gives you a burst of steam, it will fuse the layers without flattening the batt.

Polyester batting is not a good choice for reversible quilts. It is slippery, and there is a greater chance of puckering or pleating when machine quilting without basting. Another, more important, reason is that if you have a dark color on one side of your quilt and a very light color on the other, you will get "shadowing" through polyester batting. Cotton, on the other hand, allows less light through, so the darker color will not affect the lighter color on the other side.

DESIGN WALL

I strongly believe that you cannot design a quilt on a horizontal surface. Most painters work on an upright easel. (I know Jackson Pollock is an exception, but that had to be because when he threw the paint on his canvas, it would have dribbled down the wall if it had been vertical.) I think you have a better chance of "seeing" your quilt develop if you put the blocks up on a design wall.

Buy some flannelette or some polyester needlepunched batting and tape or pin it to the largest wall you have access to. Or buy yourself a BlockButler, a wonderful system that allows you to put up a design wall on any surface without having to pin or tape (see "Resources" on page 94).

As you make your blocks, put them up on the wall and then get back as far as you can to look at them. If it is difficult to stand far enough back (this is a problem if your sewing space happens to be a closet), get your camera and look through the lens, or look through the wrong end of a pair of binoculars to see what your quilt looks like. You'll be surprised sometimes to see that a fabric that looked gorgeous on the machine looks washed out when you see it from a distance. It's a good idea to know this before you use a whole bunch of that fabric in your blocks and then have to rip it all out. I also find that if I live with a quilt-in-progress on the design wall for a few days, I see things I would have missed if the piece had been lying on a table.

❧ REVERSIBLE BLOCKS ❧

If you are making your first reversible quilt, I recommend making a scrap quilt. (For the uninitiated, that simply means using lots of different fabrics rather than just two or three.) You won't have to worry about running out of one fabric, and you can put small amounts of many different fabrics in your piece. If you do run out of any of them, there are lots more at your local quilt shop.

I also feel that quilts with just a few fabrics in them aren't usually as interesting as scrap quilts. I know when I started quilting I played it safe and made quite a few three-fabric quilts. You know the kind: you start with a "theme" fabric and then choose two colors from that fabric as your complements. It's safe, but it can also be boring. I kept looking at the wild and wonderful quilts in the magazines and decided that it was time to give up safe and try something more exciting.

One other thing to remember: there is no quilt sergeant out there who will make you do 100 push-ups if you break some of the "rules" when you combine fabrics. It's all right to put colors that clash together. It is also not a federal offense to use many different patterned fabrics together. Look in magazines or visit a quilt show to see how much more exciting multifabric quilts are.

Having said all of the above, if you like three-fabric quilts, then that is the right way for you to work. You are the artist—you decide what works for you.

CHOOSING THE BLOCK SIZE

My personal preference is to work in block sizes that finish at 9" or less. Anything bigger may start to look a bit clunky, or it may look like you got tired of piecing. Larger blocks are more easily distorted when you machine quilt them because they are quilted without thread basting. However, this is largely eliminated if you use a fusible batting, so you can make the block as big as you want. Personal preference plays a big role.

PREPARING BATTING SQUARES

The very first step in making a reversible block is to cut batting squares. They are your only reference point, so it's important to cut them accurately. I usually stack just two layers of batting when I'm cutting to avoid the distortion you get when you try to cut too many layers at once.

Cut the batting squares an inch larger than your desired finished block. If you want your finished block to be 8" square (after it's sewn into your quilt), cut your batting squares 9" x 9". This gives you ½" for your seam allowance, and the other ½" is your little insurance policy. This will allow you to trim each of the blocks to the exact size you want them to be.

CUTTING TRIANGLES

The basic block consists of a half-square triangle and a set of strips on each side (front and reverse) of the block. For the triangles, cut squares first and then cut the squares once diagonally to make half-square triangles. The size of this square should be ⅜" larger than the batting square. So, for an 8" finished block, cut the squares for the triangles 9⅜" x 9⅜".

I wouldn't recommend using directional fabrics in your first reversible quilt. If you do use them for the triangles, you must be careful how you cut them because the stripe will be going in opposite directions. One way would be to fussy cut each one using a triangle ruler of an appropriate size. Another way is to put two squares wrong sides together and make the diagonal cut in the same direction every time. This gives you stripes that will be going in the right direction.

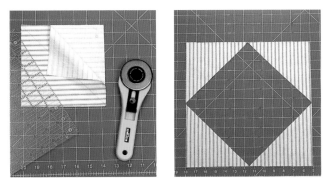

Place two squares wrong sides together with the stripes going horizontally. Cut on the diagonal in the same direction for each pair of squares.

CUTTING STRIPS

You can use strips of any width in your reversible blocks. Use strips from your scrap basket and cut new strips as needed. My favorite sizes are between 1¼" and 2¼" wide. When cutting strips from yardage, cut a narrow, a medium, and a wide strip across the width of each of your fabrics. There's no need to cut specific strip lengths. You can place the entire strip on the batting, then sew, flip, and trim the excess.

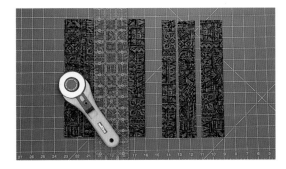

Strip widths are entirely up to you. It is not necessary to match them with each other or from block to block. In fact, I strongly recommend that you not try to match them. Random is better. Because of the way blocks are trimmed later, the finished size of the last strip, which ends up looking like a small triangle, can vary as much as half an inch from block to block.

ASSEMBLING THE BASIC BLOCK

Now you are ready to make your first block. You should have a stack of batting squares in addition to triangles and strips for both sides of your quilt, referred to as side A and side B.

1. Put an 80/12 Universal needle in your machine and thread it with 50/3 medium gray cotton thread. For the bobbin, use a thread that looks good on the fabric you have chosen for the large triangles on side B of your block. When you sew strips on side A, the bobbin thread is quilting side B.

Bobbin Thread

If the two sides of your block are similar in color, you can probably use the same bobbin thread for both sides. If you have two very distinct color schemes, however, you will need to use two different bobbin threads, one to match side A and one to match side B. If you are using a multicolored fabric on either side, it might be difficult to find a thread to match. In that case, I would use invisible thread in the bobbin.

2. Put the walking foot on your machine.

3. Starting with side A, place a large triangle, right side up, on a batting square so that the long side of the triangle (the hypotenuse) is ¼" beyond an imaginary diagonal line running from corner to corner. Or draw a diagonal line ¼" away from the center (see "Optional Placement Line" on page 15).

Check ¼" seam allowance by looking underneath the batting square.

4. For the first strip, I recommend a wide strip rather than a narrow one. Often, while getting a perfect ¼" seam allowance on the side you are sewing, you may get a wider seam allowance on the other side of the block. This is not a mistake. The extra seam allowance doesn't matter as long as the strip is wide enough to look good. Place the first strip on the edge of the triangle with right sides together. Make sure you can see at least one thread of the triangle fabric beneath your

strip. This will ensure that the triangle doesn't slip beneath the strip (where you can't see it) and miss being caught in the seam.

5. Carefully turn the square over, making sure the triangle and strip don't move. Place a large triangle on the opposite corner of the batting square on side B; place a wide strip on the triangle with right sides together just as you did on side A. The two triangles should be on opposite sides and opposite corners of the batting square.

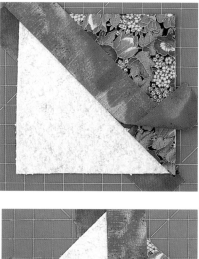

6. Pin the strips and triangles on the stitching line. Normally, you pin at right angles to the stitching line, but for this technique, place the pins *on* the stitching line. This will show you if you have an adequate seam allowance on the other side. Turn the block over and check. If the seam allowance isn't adequate, take the pins out and rearrange the pieces until you have at least ¼" on both sides.

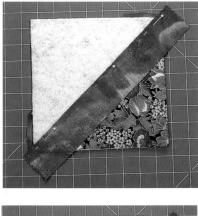

7. If you are using fusible batting, you may want to fuse the triangles to the batting for added stability.

8. Sew through all layers using a scant ¼" seam allowance. If the seam allowance is wider than ¼" on the side you are sewing, it will be too narrow on the other side. This is the only time you need to use a scant seam allowance; sew all other strips with a standard ¼" seam allowance.

Optional Placement Line

Over the course of teaching the reversible-quilts technique, I have found that many students like the added step of drawing a guideline on the batting to make lining up the first strip on both sides easier. I don't do it because it takes too long and adds another step. However, anything that improves the results is a benefit. So if it makes it easier and saves you time or eliminates frustration, by all means use it.

1. With a see-through ruler and a pencil or washable marking pen, draw a line ¼" from the diagonal on side A of your batting square.

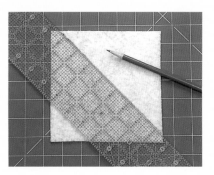

2. On side B, draw a line ¼" from the opposite side of the diagonal. Use these lines to position the triangle; then continue with step 4 of the basic instructions on page 14.

9. Open the strip and finger-press the seam; repeat for the other side. I like to finger-press so that the batting is not flattened by an iron. Be sure to finger-press the corners well. If there is a little pleat near the corners, it will throw off the diagonal, which is what you will use later as a reference point to square up the block. If you have used a 42"-long strip, trim the excess off so you aren't struggling with long tails.

10. Up to this point, none of the thread is visible; it's enclosed in the seam on both sides. But when you add the next strip, the bobbin thread will be visible on the other side. Make sure you have a compatible thread in the bobbin.

11. Choose the second strip for side A. It can be any width you want. Place it right sides together on the first strip, lining up the end with the edge of the batting square, not with the end of the first strip. Sew with a standard ¼" seam allowance. Open the strip and finger-press.

12. Continue adding strips to side A until the batting square is almost covered. When you are one strip from the end, choose a wide strip again. If the last strip is too narrow, there will be hardly anything left when the block is trimmed and joined with other blocks later.

13. Turn your block over. Make sure your bobbin thread is compatible with side A and add strips on side B to cover the batting square.

14. When both sides of the batting square are covered with strips, it's time to square up the block by trimming the edges. Place your block on the cutting mat, with the diagonal seams going toward the upper right if you are right-handed or upper left if you are left-handed. With a see-through square ruler at least as big as your block, place the diagonal line of the ruler on the center diagonal seam between the triangle and the first strip.

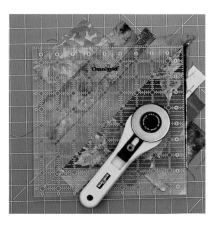

15. With the 1" marks of the ruler in the upper right corner (upper left if you are left-handed), move the ruler until you come almost to the edge of the fabric on the right-hand side and the top of the block. Trim the

side and then the top. You'll be trimming the minimum amount on these first two cuts so that if there's a problem when you turn the block over, you can do the first cuts over again.

16. Now turn the block over so that the center diagonal seam is facing the same direction as before.

17. Place the diagonal line of the ruler on the center diagonal seam as you did for the first side. Keeping the diagonal line of the ruler on the center diagonal seam, move the ruler until the desired measurements on the ruler are on the previously cut edges. For example, if your blocks will be 6" finished, align the 6½" horizontal and vertical marks on the ruler with the cut edges; the extra ½" is for seam allowances. When you have the sides positioned at the appropriate measurements, trim the remaining edges of the block.

18. Place the blocks on your design wall as you complete them.

Fixing a Bare Corner

Don't worry if there's a corner of batting showing after you add your last strip. You'll be trimming quite a bit off when you square up the block, and chances are your little bit of "slip showing" will disappear then. If not, sew a small piece of the same fabric to the corner to cover the batting.

BLOCK VARIATIONS

You will soon see that many variations are possible with the reversible-quilt technique. I used to say that anything that looks good when joined with a sashing strip could be made as a reversible quilt. Now, I'm even challenging that assumption. If you treat a pieced block as sashing, you can even make reversible quilts that look like they are made without any sashing (see "From the Freezer" on page 41).

Block Variation 1

Use two triangles on one side. This is even simpler than the basic block (see the corner squares on the border of side B of "Jean's Star" on page 79). Instead of adding a strip onto the first triangle, place another triangle on top with right sides together. Then turn the block over and treat the other side in any way you wish. When using two triangles on one side, it is best to sew from that side, because occasionally you get an extra-wide seam allowance on the side you can't see. If you get a wider seam allowance when using strips, it doesn't matter; you can just add another strip. However, if you get a wider seam allowance on a side with triangles, your triangle ends up being too small to cover the batting square. If you choose to use two triangles on both sides of your block, be extremely careful to sew a scant ¼" seam allowance.

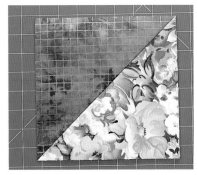

Two Triangles

Block Variation 2

Use all strips on one side (see side B of "Altered Amish" on page 85). Place two strips right sides together instead of one strip and a large triangle. Just remember to place the edges of the strips ¼" beyond the imaginary diagonal line running from corner to corner on the batting square, or draw a placement line. (See "Optional Placement Line" on page 15).

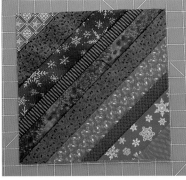

All Strips

Block Variation 3

Use an accent strip in the center of each block. This is very similar to block variation 2. Center the accent piece directly on the diagonal of the block; then continue adding strips as in variation 2 (see side B of "Altered Amish" on page 85 for an example).

Center Accent Strip

Block Variation 4

Use a pieced triangle and one large triangle.

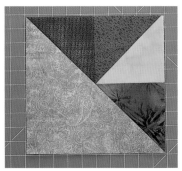

One Triangle and One Pieced Triangle

Block Variation 5

Use one piece of fabric. This one is the easiest of all. Simply place a piece of fabric the same size as the batting square on one side (see side A of "Altered Amish" on page 85 and side B of "Log Cabin by the Lake" on page 75).

Place the square of fabric, right side up, on the batting square and turn the block over. Depending on what you put on the other side, it may be necessary to add some quilting lines to anchor the batting. Always quilt as you go.

Fusible batting would be a good choice for this variation.

One Piece of Fabric—Too Beautiful to Cut

Block Variation 6

Use a prepieced or appliquéd block on one side. This is, in effect, a variation on block variation 5 (see "From the Freezer" on page 41).

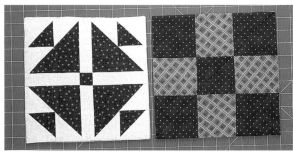

Pieced Blocks

Block Variation 7

Piece directly onto a square of batting, without a backing fabric. This is another situation where fusible batting would be a good choice (see side B of "Not Enough Cats" on page 89). Use this option when you will be adding a completed block to the reverse side and then quilting it.

Piecing without Backing

Block Variation 8

This is very similar to block variation 7, but instead of piecing directly onto the batting, you will be quilting on the batting without a backing fabric. This is a good solution when you do not want quilting stitches on the reverse side. Use fusible batting for this variation. When the quilting is done, the block is then fused to whatever you are putting on the other side (see "Peace, Health, and Happiness" on page 69 and "Nana Loves Emma" on page 51).

Quilting without Backing

Block Variation 9

Setting and corner triangles are another place to use fusible batting, if you wish. Layer a fusible-batting triangle between side A and side B triangles and quilt as desired. For setting triangles, trim only the two short sides; for corner triangles, trim only the long side. After the quilt is assembled, the remaining sides will be trimmed.

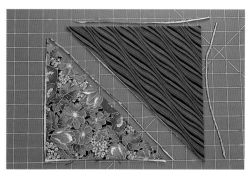

Setting and Corner Triangles

❧ Sashing ❧

Sashing is composed of strips that join the blocks, rows, and borders. It performs two tasks: it is a functional piece that joins the blocks, and it is also a design element. Your choice of fabric for sashing can make a strong statement, as the lime green does on side B of "Altered Amish" on page 85, or it can make almost no statement, completely disappearing as you can see on both sides of "Nana Loves Emma" on page 51. Sashing can tone down a quilt that's too busy or liven up a quilt that's leaning toward boring. The fabric you use for sashing can be the same throughout the quilt, or it can change from block to block (see side A of "Jean's Star" on page 79).

In this book, I've gone even further and introduced the use of a pieced block as sashing. Both sides of "From the Freezer" on page 41 make use of 4"-wide sashing. Side A uses a pieced block, and side B uses a solid block; both sides look as if they were made without any sashing at all. I think this opens up all sorts of possibilities for quilts that were previously considered unlikely candidates for the reversible technique.

Sashing Choices

When I am satisfied with the setting of the blocks on my design wall, I audition fabrics I think will work as sashing. If I have lots of a particular fabric, I don't mind wasting a small piece, so I cut a strip about ⅝" wide—the width of the finished sashing.

Cut strips from as many fabrics as you wish to audition. Lay the strips, one at a time, on the blocks to see how each one looks. Don't forget to stand as far back as you can to see the effect of the color on your quilt.

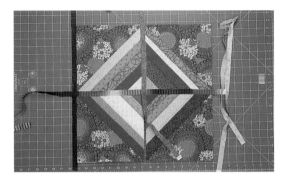

If you have a limited amount of fabric and would rather not waste a piece for auditioning, remove at least four blocks from the design wall, being careful to note their positions. Place the potential sashing fabric on the wall. Then place the four blocks on the sashing fabric, with approximately ⅝" space between them. Keep auditioning fabrics until you find the one that looks best with the blocks.

Don't forget that you must audition sashing fabrics for both sides of the quilt. Occasionally, one fabric will work for both sides, but more often than not, you'll need to pick two different fabrics.

BASIC SASHING

Basic sashing finishes at ⅝" wide on both sides of the quilt. You will cut strips of different widths, however, for the two different sides—1⅛" wide for one side and 1¾" wide for the other. It doesn't matter on which side you use the two widths, unless you're doing a pieced sashing (see "Pieced Sashing" on page 22).

1. Cut 1⅛"-wide strips from one sashing fabric, and then cut 1¾"-wide strips from the other sashing fabric. Cut across the full width of your fabric.

2. Fold the 1¾" strips in half lengthwise, wrong sides together, and press.

3. Use the full length of the strips. On side A, align the raw edges of the folded strip with the raw edges of the first block to be joined. On side B, align the raw edge of the 1⅛"-wide strip with the raw edges of the same block, right sides together. Sew both sashing strips to the first block with a ¼" seam. You are sewing both sashing strips to the same block at the same time.

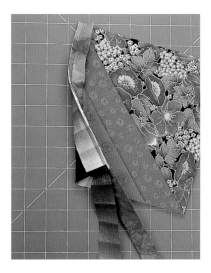

4. Trim the ends of the strips even with the top and bottom of the block.

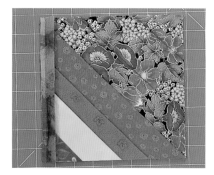

5. Sew the second block to the raw edge of the 1⅛"-wide strip.

Note: The edges of the two seam allowances should meet in the middle of the sashing strip and fill the space between the two blocks. If there is a gap between the two edges, increase your seam allowance; if the two edges overlap, decrease your seam allowance.

6. Continue sewing sashing strips between blocks until you finish the row. You now have three of the four edges of the sashing strips sewn by machine. Pin the folded strip in

place, covering the machine stitching. Sew the remaining folded edge by hand or machine (see "Finishing the Sashing by Machine" on page 23).

7. To join the rows or to add a border, follow the same directions as for joining block to block but use longer sashing strips. If you need to piece sashing strips, sew the ends together with a diagonal seam. Trim the excess fabric and press the seam open.

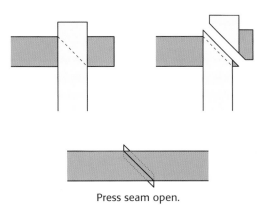

Press seam open.

8. When joining horizontal rows of blocks, be sure to line up the vertical strips between the blocks from one row to the next.

PIECED SASHING

The lime green star on side B of "Altered Amish" on page 85 was created by piecing the sashing, when necessary, to continue the design. Although I have used pieced sashing on the folded side, I recommend using it only on the single-layer side (using 1⅛"-wide strips) whenever possible because it is much easier to work with and less bulky.

For vertical sashing, you can sew different-colored strips between the blocks as described above. To use different colors in the horizontal sashing, you need to join the different colors before sewing the sashing to a row of blocks. In a perfect world, you would be able to precut strips to match the size of your blocks; for example, you would cut strips 8½" long if you are working with 8" finished blocks. However, this isn't a perfect world, and I don't know about your piecing, but mine isn't always perfect. So rather than precut the sashing pieces to what they should be, I cut strips a little longer and join them one by one, measuring from block to block. This may sound a little tedious, but the results are worth it. Let's see how this is done for a navy blue block with a lime green sashing strip used to continue a design line, as in side B of "Altered Amish" on page 85.

1. Measure the distance for the first piece of horizontal sashing—in this case, lime green—and cut it a little longer. Then measure the navy blue blocks and cut a navy blue strip a little longer.

2. Sew the green and navy blue strips together, end to end.

3. Pin the joined strips to the blocks, making sure the seam is aligned with the vertical seam between the blue and green fabrics. Now carefully smooth the blue fabric on top of the blue blocks and make a fold at the next

seam between the blue and green fabrics. Finger-press the fold.

4. Measure the next section for the lime green sashing and cut a piece a little longer. Sew the next green strip to the blue strip exactly on the fold. Pin this portion of the sashing to the row of blocks.

5. Continue in this manner, measuring, cutting, stitching, and pinning until you have completed the horizontal sashing for the row. Sew the sashing to the row of blocks.

Finishing the Sashing by Machine

If you choose to sew the remaining side of the sashing by machine, my favorite way is to set the machine to a very narrow zigzag stitch. Thread the machine with 60/2 cotton thread that matches the sashing fabric and use a 60/8 needle and invisible nylon thread in the bobbin.

Pin the folded strip in place and sew along the folded edge.

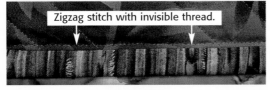

Bobbin Side

Another option is to set the machine to do a decorative stitch and use a decorative thread in both top and bottom. This is particularly nice on a binding.

WIDE SASHING

Wide sashing can be any width you want. It can be 2" wide as in "Not Enough Cats" on page 89 or 4" wide as in "From the Freezer" on page 41 (see sashing details on page 45). As an example, let's say that you would like 4" sashing.

1. Cut 4½"-wide strips from both side A and side B sashing fabrics (or use a pieced strip such as flying geese). Using the strips from one sashing fabric, turn one long edge under ¼" and press. Sew the unfolded raw edges of the strips to the raw edges of the front and back of the block at the same time. Trim the ends of the strips even with the top and bottom of the block.

2. Sew the next block to the strip that doesn't have the edge turned under.

3. Measure the distance between the two seam allowances and cut a strip of batting that wide. Lay the batting in the space and hand stitch or machine stitch the folded edge down.

4. To hold the batting in place, quilt the sashing strip as you complete each row.

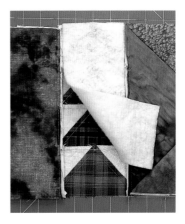

❧ BORDERS ❧

Borders on reversible quilts are joined to the quilt with sashing strips, just as rows of blocks are joined together. The sashing fabric used to join a border to a quilt can be the same as the border fabric or a contrasting fabric. If you use a contrasting fabric, the sashing will look like an inner border. If you use the same fabric, it just disappears. It all depends on the look you want.

BASIC BORDERS

I cut borders 1" wider and longer than the desired finished size—½" for seam allowances and ½" to allow for any slippage when quilting.

1. Measure the length of your quilt through the center. Add an extra 1" in both directions.

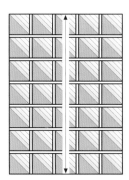

For borders, measure
through center of quilt.

2. Cut border strips for each side of the quilt according to your measurements. Cut strips of batting the same size.

3. If you are using fusible batting, fuse the three layers together. If you are using regular batting, pin or spray-baste the three layers together with the batting in the middle.

4. Quilt as desired.

5. Trim to the desired length and width, leaving ½" for seam allowances.

6. Join border strips to the sides of the quilt with sashing strips, as you do for blocks and rows (see "Basic Sashing" on page 21 if needed).

7. Measure the width through the center, add an extra 1" in both directions, and repeat steps 2–6 to add the top and bottom borders.

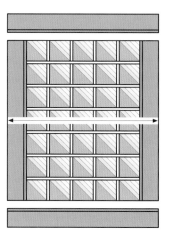

BORDERS WITH CORNER SQUARES

1. Measure the length and width of your quilt through the center. Add an extra 1" for seam allowances and to allow for any slippage when quilting.

2. Follow steps 2–6 for "Basic Borders" to add borders to the sides of the quilt.

3. Cut corner squares to the size needed plus an extra 1" and layer with batting.

4. Quilt the corner squares, trim to the desired size leaving ½" for seam allowances, and sew them to the ends of the remaining borders with pieces of sashing. Join the top and bottom borders to the quilt with sashing strips.

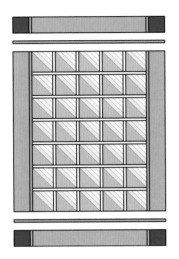

BORDERS WITH A CONTRASTING INNER BORDER

In "Nana Loves Emma" on page 51, you'll see that the sashing that joins the border to the quilt looks like an inner border. To achieve this look, join the top and bottom border strips to the quilt, using a contrasting fabric for the sashing. For the sides, sew a rectangle of border fabric to each end of a side sashing strip, referring to "Pieced Sashing" on page 22. Sew the side border strips to the quilt with the pieced sashing strips.

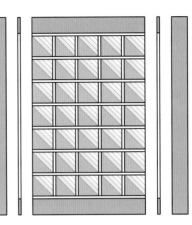

Enlarging a Quilt

I was recently asked if there was any way to make a quilt larger after it had been quilted and bound. It appears that a child had "graduated" from a youth bed to a larger bed and her quilt was no longer big enough. I suggested that the binding be removed and a border be added with sashing, using one of the techniques above. You would need to add a new binding because the quilt would be bigger, but that's a lot easier than making a whole new quilt.

❧ BINDING AND FINISHING ❧

*B*inding need not be just the "tidying up" bit at the end of making a quilt. Like sashing, it can play a decorative as well as a functional role. In some quilts, you may want the binding to just disappear, while in others you may want it to make a bold statement. If you are lucky, the same fabric will work on both sides. If so, follow the "Basic Binding" instructions below. If not, see "Reversible Binding" on page 28. Yardage requirements for both basic binding and reversible binding are provided with each quilt project.

BASIC BINDING

This binding is the same as I would use on a nonreversible quilt. I was taught this method shortly after I learned to quilt and have always loved it. It makes a beautiful finished corner on both sides of the quilt; each side will have perfect, machine-sewn miters. If you haven't done binding this way, give it a try. I like it because the two ends of the binding are enclosed in a corner so there is no need to do that horrible thing with joining the ends, which always looks messy when I try it.

From the width of the fabric, cut enough 2½"-wide strips to go around all sides of the quilt plus 8" extra for joining strips and turning corners. Join the strips end to end to make a long continuous strip. Join them with a diagonal seam as you did for long sashing strips (see page 22 for details if needed).

1. Fold the strip in half lengthwise, wrong sides together, and press.

2. Put the walking foot on your machine.

3. Starting at a corner and leaving a 2" tail, match the raw edges of the binding with the raw edges of the quilt. Beginning ¼" from the corner, anchor your stitches and sew the binding to the first side of the quilt with a ¼" seam allowance. Stop ¼" from the corner and again anchor your stitches.

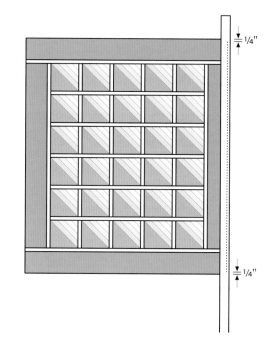

4. Remove the quilt from the machine. Draw a perpendicular line from the stitching line (A) to the fold (C). I call this the baseline.

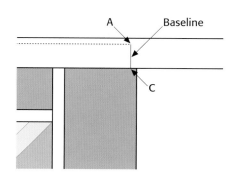

5. Measure the distance from the stitching line to the folded edge of your binding strip. It should be 1". Find the center of the baseline (it should be ½" from the folded edge and the stitching line) and make a mark. From that mark, measure ½" to the right of the baseline, and make another mark (B). Draw a line from points A and C to point B to form a triangle.

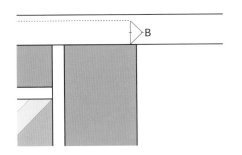

6. Fold the binding under at point B. Pin in place. If you can't see the triangle you've just drawn and the folded edges are not aligned, it's folded the wrong way. Starting with the needle at point A, anchor your stitches. Then sew to point B, pivot, and sew to point C; anchor your stitches. Do not sew across the baseline.

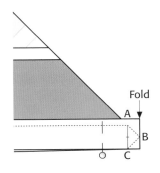

7. Remove the quilt from the machine and align the binding with the edge of the next side of the quilt. Mark the point at which you start stitching point D; this is under point A. With the needle at point D, anchor your stitches and then sew to ¼" from the next corner, anchoring your stitches.

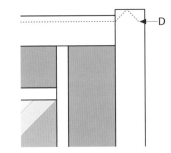

8. Repeat steps 4–7 for the second and third corners. On the fourth side, sew to where you started (¼" from the end of side 4); anchor your stitches. Draw the ABC triangle as you did for the previous three corners, but instead of folding the binding under, pin it to the tail you left at the beginning, aligning the folded edges.

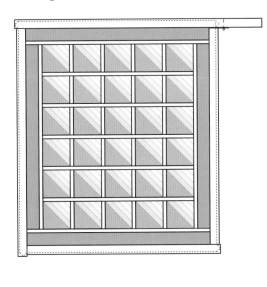

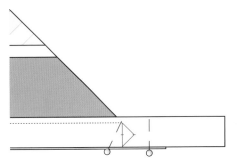

9. Sew the triangle through both pieces of binding, thereby enclosing the ends in the corner seam.

10. Trim the corners from each triangle and turn right side out. This will give you a mitered corner on both sides of your quilt.

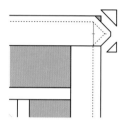

11. Turn the binding to the reverse side and hand or machine sew the folded edge to the quilt.

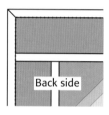

Back side

Note: If you want to use strips wider than 2½" for your binding, the technique will still work. After folding and sewing the binding to the quilts, measure the distance between the stitching line and the folded edge (step 5) and divide the measurement in half. Use this measurement to mark the point of the triangle (B).

REVERSIBLE BINDING

But what if the same binding fabric just won't do for both sides of the quilt? Reversible binding is easy to do, but you cannot do a mitered corner as you did for the basic binding. Instead, you will sew the binding to the sides first and then to the top and bottom edges.

1. From the width of the fabric, cut enough 1⅛"-wide strips to go around the quilt plus a few inches for the corners. Cut strips for the other side 1¾" wide. (This is ⅛" wider than the instructions in *Reversible Quilts*. It makes

very little difference, and it's easier to remember this width; it corresponds with the cutting for ⅝" sashing.) It does not matter on which side you use the two widths; as an example, in these instructions, the narrower strip will go on the front of the quilt. If the sides of the quilt are longer than 40", join the strips end to end with a diagonal seam as you do when piecing sashing (see page 22).

2. Fold the 1¾"-wide strip in half lengthwise, wrong sides together, and press.

3. With right sides together and matching raw edges, sew the single layer of binding and the folded layer of binding together with a ¼"-wide seam allowance.

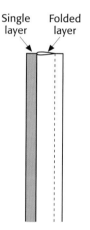

Single   Folded
layer   layer

4. Press the seam open. This helps the binding fold at the midpoint when you attach the binding to the quilt.

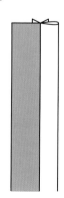

5. Sew the binding to opposite edges of the quilt first. With right sides together and raw edges matching, sew the single layer of

binding to one side of the quilt. Trim the ends even with the quilt. Fold the binding at the seam line and hand or machine sew the folded edge to the reverse side of the quilt.

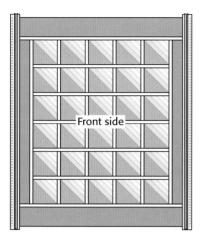

Front side

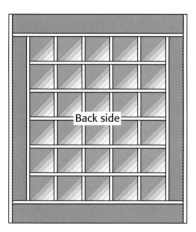

Back side

6. Leaving a ½" tail at the beginning and end, sew the single layer of binding to the remaining edges of the quilt.

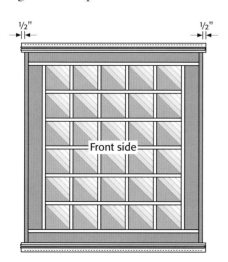

½"　　　½"

Front side

7. With right sides together, sew the ends of the binding flush with the ends of the quilt. Make sure you keep the folded edge lined up with the folded edge of the seam allowance you have just sewn on. Trim the seam allowance and turn right sides out.

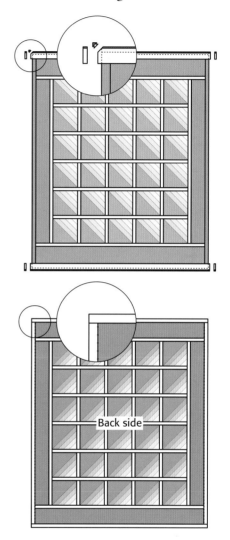

Back side

8. Hand or machine sew the folded edge to the reverse side of the quilt as you did with the first two sides.

LABELS

Where do you put a label on a reversible quilt? Unless you can incorporate it into a block on one side of the quilt, I suggest you put it on the binding.

My sewing machine has an embroidered alphabet, so I "typed" my name, where I live, and the current year into the memory. When I prepare my bindings, I sew this information onto the folded side before I sew the binding to the quilt.

HANGING SLEEVE

This method was created by Sharron Evans, who has generously agreed to share it with us. It is the only way to have a regulation-type hanging sleeve on a reversible quilt that doesn't interfere with the top 4" of one side of it. It is not sewn to either side of the quilt, but is attached "between" the bindings and extends above the quilt. Even if you are planning on using basic binding on your quilt—where you would normally use a 2½"-wide strip folded in half lengthwise—you will have to cut two pieces (of the same fabric if desired) so that the sleeve can be sewn to the quilt with the binding. The other three sides of the quilt will be bound in the usual fashion.

1. Measure from side to side along the top edge of the quilt and subtract 2".

2. Cut a piece of fabric 8½" wide and the length determined in step 1. Turn under and hem the two short ends. This will produce the 4" hanging sleeve usually required for quilt shows.

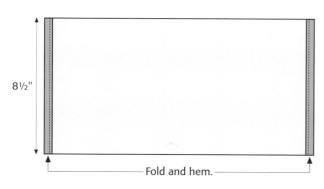

8½"

Fold and hem.

Make It Black

If you are entering your quilt in a show, you might want to make the hanging sleeve from black fabric so it blends in with the black drapes often used at shows.

3. Fold lengthwise, wrong sides together, and press.

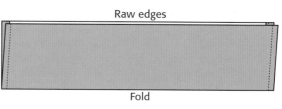

Raw edges

Fold

4. Measure the top of the quilt and add 1". Cut two pieces of binding, one 1⅛" by the length you have determined and the other one 1¾" by the same length. Fold the 1¾" strip in half lengthwise with wrong sides together and press. Even if you are planning on using the same fabric to bind both sides of your quilt, you will have to cut two pieces as if you were making a reversible binding.

5. Center the sleeve on the folded binding strip lining up the raw edges. With right sides together, center the 1⅛" binding strip on the other side of the hanging sleeve, matching raw edges. Sew the two pieces of binding to the sleeve.

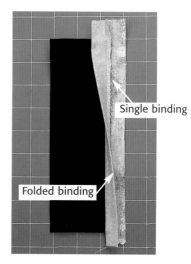

Single binding

Folded binding

6. With the single thickness, sew the sleeve to the top of your quilt.

7. Hand or machine finish the folded edge just as you would with the folded edge of sashing or binding.

8. Bind the other three sides, following "Basic Binding" on page 26 or "Reversible Binding" on page 28.

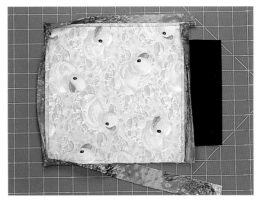

Reversible Binding

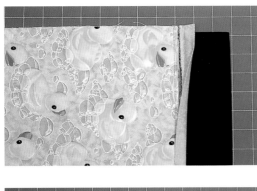

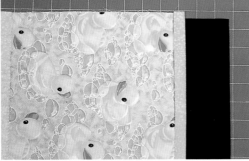

Basic Binding

THE QUILT PROJECTS

*T*he materials list for each project is based on 42"-wide fabric, with 40" of usable fabric after washing. It's difficult to provide yardage requirements for some of the quilts because they use many different fabrics. When you see the phrase "total of assorted prints," it means that you need a combination of scraps, strips, and leftover pieces to total the amount given.

I've provided yardage amounts for sashing in both widths that you'll need to cut. Basic sashing always finishes at ⅝" on each side. I've also included binding amounts for basic binding and reversible binding. Basic binding is based on cutting 2½"-wide strips.

If you want to use the same fabric for any of the various parts of the quilt, simply add the yardages together and buy the total amount.

Table runner: 14½" x 40" • Finished block: 9" x 9"
Made by Sharon Pederson

Side A: Autumn Leaves   **Side B: Spring Flowers**

THE SALTED PEANUT TABLE RUNNER

When *Reversible Quilts* came out, I was inundated with requests for something quick to use as a class sample. It just so happened that I also needed a small gift for someone. She wouldn't dream of putting a quilt on the wall, so that eliminated a wall hanging.

Hmmm . . . table runners are small, I thought; I'll make her a table runner. After making about six of them, I was still thinking of fabrics to use for another one! I decided we should call this the "Salted Peanut Table Runner," because you can't make just one. They are lots of fun to make and go together so quickly you can make half a dozen of them in no time at all.

In this table runner, the setting-triangle fabric is the one that you see the most. I usually choose it first and then fill in the block fabrics. There are approximately 20 strips of varying widths on each side of the table runner, and some of them are quite short, so you won't need much of any particular fabric to make one up. It's a great way to use up those bits and pieces that are left over from other projects.

MATERIALS

Yardages are based on 42"-wide fabrics.

Side A
- ½ yard of black print for block triangles
- 1 fat quarter* of gold print for setting triangles
- ⅛ yard *each* of assorted prints for blocks:
  2 red, 2 yellow, 2 green, 2 gold, and 2 orange
  (20 strips total of varying widths)

Side B
- ½ yard of floral print for block triangles
- 1 fat quarter* of green striped fabric for setting triangles
- ⅛ yard *each* of assorted prints for blocks:
  2 pink, 2 yellow, 2 blue, 2 green, and 2 purple
  (20 strips total of varying widths)

Basic Sashing
- ⅛ yard for 1⅛"-wide strips
- ¼ yard for 1¾"-wide strips

Basic Binding
- ⅜ yard

Reversible Binding
- ¼ yard for 1⅛"-wide strips
- ¼ yard for 1¾"-wide strips

Batting
- ⅓ yard of 96"-wide batting

Purchase more fabric if you wish to fussy cut.

Directional Fabrics

To use a directional fabric to its best advantage, I usually fussy cut the setting triangles so I have all of the stripes or design images going the same way.

CUTTING

From the batting, cut:

3 squares, 10" x 10"

2 squares, 10½" x 10½"; cut once on the diagonal to yield 4 triangles. *Or*, if you have a large-enough piece, cut 1 square, 14" x 14"; cut twice on the diagonal to yield 4 triangles.

From the black print, cut:

2 squares, 10⅜" x 10⅜"; cut once on the diagonal to yield 4 triangles. (You will use only 3.)

From the floral print, cut:

2 squares, 10⅜" x 10⅜"; cut once on the diagonal to yield 4 triangles. (You will use only 3.)

From the assorted prints for sides A and B, cut:

Narrow, medium, and wide strips as needed

From the gold print*, cut:

1 square, 14" x 14"; cut twice on the diagonal to yield 4 setting triangles

From the green striped fabric*, cut:

1 square, 14" x 14"; cut twice on the diagonal to yield 4 setting triangles

*If you are fussy cutting, make a template the same size as your batting triangles and cut four triangles.

ASSEMBLY

1. Referring to "Reversible Blocks" on page 12, make three blocks. Trim to 9½" x 9½".

2. Referring to "Block Variation 9" on page 19, make four setting triangles; trim only the two short sides. There will be very little to trim off; basically, you are just tidying up the edges.

3. Referring to "Basic Sashing" on page 21, cut sashing strips for sides A and B. Join the blocks and rows as shown in the diagram.

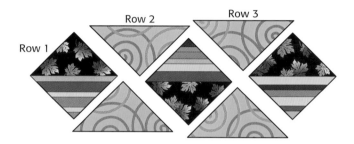

4. Trim the long sides of the setting triangles and round the corners if desired. Rounding the corners will make the binding go on easier.

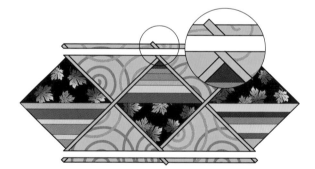

Trim ¼" beyond points.

Round corners if desired.

Easy Mitered Binding

When mitering corners that are greater than 90°, such as the points on this table runner, I love the binding miter tool made by Jackie Robinson. It is a terrific little ruler that makes these miters a breeze. See "Resources" on page 94.

5. Referring to "Basic Binding" on page 26 or "Reversible Binding" on page 28, cut strips and bind the edges of the quilt.

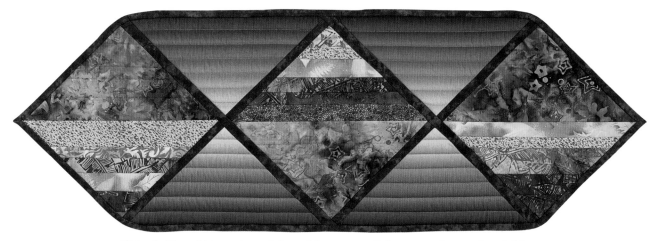

Side A: For this version of the table runner, I fussy cut the gradated fabric so that the color placement in each triangle would match.

Side B

Quilt: 40" x 60" • Finished block: 9½" x 9½"
Made by Sharon Pederson

Side A: Rail Fence

Side B: Checkerboard

THE FASTEST-EVER CHARITY QUILT

Quilters are some of the most generous people on earth. They give so much of their time (and their stash) to disadvantaged groups in their communities—I am constantly amazed at how quickly the quilts arrive after a tragedy. The numbers of quilts made for donation and charities are staggering.

Now, making a quilt using the reversible technique is pretty quick, but a friend of mine has developed an even quicker way. LaVerne Somerville is a talented quilter who lives in my part of the world; she has often organized groups to make quilts for special-needs babies or patients in long-term care facilities. She has the wonderful ability to look at a quilt and figure out a way to make it easier; that is exactly what she did with the reversible technique. To finish in record time, this quilt is completely machine sewn; there isn't a hand stitch anywhere. When you have to get something made yesterday, this quilt makes it possible.

The backs of these quilts are just that—backs—unless you decide to have fun with them as I did. I couldn't resist doing something a little different on that side, too.

MATERIALS
Yardages are based on 42"-wide fabrics.

Side A
- ⅝ yard *each* of 5 different fabrics for Rail Fence blocks

Side B
- 1 yard of blue print fabric for blocks
- 1 yard of white print fabric for blocks

Basic Sashing
- ⅜ yard for 1⅛"-wide strips
- ⅝ yard for 1¾"-wide strips

Basic Binding
- ⅜ yard

Reversible Binding
- ¼ yard for 1⅛"-wide strips
- ⅜ yard for 1¾"-wide strips

Batting
- 1 yard of 96"-wide batting

CUTTING

From the batting cut:
6 pieces, 10½" x 42"

From *each* of the 5 fabrics for side A, cut:
6 strips, 2½" x 42"

From *each* of the blue and white prints, cut:
3 strips, 10½" x 42"

BLOCK ASSEMBLY

1. Place one side B strip, right side down, on your work surface and cover with a batting piece.

2. Lining up the raw edges with the left side of the batting, place two fabric strips for side A, right sides together, on the batting and pin.

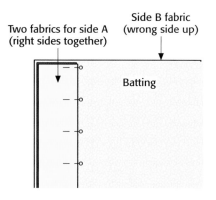

3. Sew with a ¼" seam through all thicknesses; flip and finger-press open.

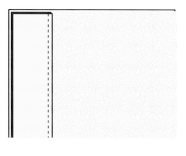

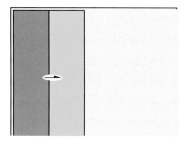

4. Repeat with the remaining side A fabrics. Make six of these strips, three with blue fabric on the back and three with white. Keep the fabric strips in the same order for each.

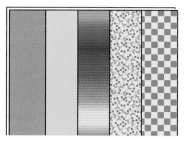

5. Trim the long sides. There will be very little to trim; essentially, you are just tidying up. Set aside the three strips with blue fabric on the back.

6. Referring to "Basic Sashing" on page 21, cut sashing strips for sides A and B. Sew sashing strips to the pieces with white fabric on the back as shown. Sew sashing strips to both sides of one strip, the left side only of another, and to the right side only of the third. Remember, you are sewing sashing strips for both side A and side B at the same time.

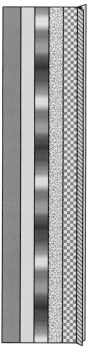

Both Sides   Left Side Only   Right Side Only

7. Trim the selvages off the end of all six strips and cut into 10" squares. You should get four from each strip for a total of 24.

8. Cut two additional 10" sashing strips for both sides A and B. Sew one set of strips to a block with sashing only on the left as shown. Sew the other strips to a block with sashing only on the right.

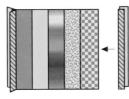

Add sashing to right side
of 1 block.

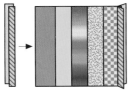

Add sashing to left side
of 1 block.

9. Make a total of 24 blocks as shown.

Make 6 with
white fabric on back.

Make 3 with
white fabric on back.

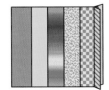

Make 3 with
white fabric on back.

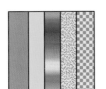

Make 12 with
blue fabric on back.

QUILT ASSEMBLY

1. On a design wall, arrange the blocks, alternating the blocks with sashing and the blocks without as shown in the quilt diagram.

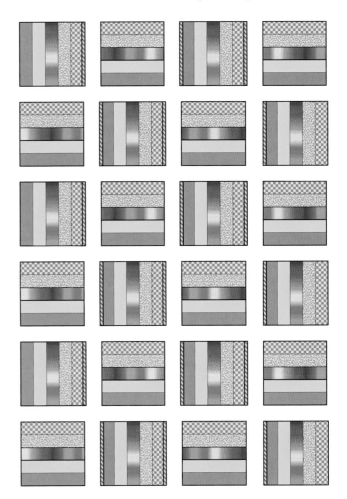

2. Refer to "Basic Sashing" on page 21 to join the blocks and rows together.

3. Referring to "Basic Binding" on page 26 or "Reversible Binding" on page 28, cut strips and bind the edges of the quilt.

Quilt: 44½" x 44½" • Finished block: 9" x 9"
Made by Sharon Pederson

Side A: Hen and Chicks

Side B: Quarter-Square Triangles

From the Freezer

'm sure a lot of you have containers in your freezer with spaghetti sauce or homemade soup in them. When you have time (or too many tomatoes), you make things, then freeze them to be used at a later date. And isn't it nice, when you'd rather spend one more hour sewing, to just grab one and thaw it out for an "instant" dinner? Well, I want to know why that is considered a virtue and having a pile of blocks already made up is referred to as a UFO (unfinished object)? I *like* having a pile of blocks in my studio ready to be put together at a moment's notice instead of having to start from scratch every time. So, here is a variation on our theme of reversible quilts using "frozen" blocks from my "freezer" (otherwise known as the back of the closet in my studio). I made the Hen and Chicks blocks years ago, and then changed my mind about the quilt and they got pushed aside.

In this quilt, a pieced block is used as sashing. You simply piece the blocks first and then treat them the same way as plain sashing. I think this will open up even more possibilities for amazing reversible quilts.

Materials

Yardages are based on 42"-wide fabrics.

Side A
- 1⅜ yards of blue-green print for sashing blocks and borders
- 1⅜ yards total of assorted light prints for blocks
- ¾ yard total of assorted dark prints for blocks

Side B
- ⅞ yard of print for borders
- ¼ yard *each* of assorted prints for blocks: 3 green, 3 yellow, 2 blue, 2 orange, 2 red, and 2 purple

Basic Sashing
- ¼ yard for 1⅛"-wide strips
- ⅜ yard for 1¾"-wide strips

Basic Binding
- ½ yard

Reversible Binding
- ¼ yard for 1⅛"-wide strips
- ⅜ yard for 1¾"-wide strips

Batting
- ⅞ yard of 96"-wide batting

Cutting

From the batting, cut:

9 squares, 9½" x 9½"

6 rectangles, 4" x 9½"*

2 strips, 4" x 35½"*

2 strips, 5" x 38"

2 strips, 5" x 47"

These might have to be trimmed down to 3½". It's best to wait until you need them to cut them.

From the assorted light prints for side A, cut:

24 triangles using template B on page 48

24 triangles using template B reversed

8 squares, 2½" x 2½"; cut once diagonally to yield 16 triangles

54 squares, 2⅞" x 2⅞"; cut once diagonally to yield 108 triangles

36 rectangles, 1½" x 4½"

From the assorted dark prints for side A, cut:

18 squares, 4⅞" x 4⅞"; cut once diagonally to yield 36 triangles

18 squares, 2⅞" x 2⅞"; cut once diagonally to yield 36 triangles

9 squares, 1½" x 1½"

From the blue-green print for side A, cut:

12 diamonds using template A on page 47

4 squares, 3⅜" x 3⅜"

2 strips, 5" x 38"

3 strips, 5" x 42"

From the assorted prints for side B, cut:

36 triangles using template C on page 49 (10 green, 10 yellow, 6 blue, 6 orange, 2 red, and 2 purple)

8 triangles using template D on page 48 (3 green, 3 yellow, 1 blue, and 1 orange)

12 rectangles, 4½" x 9½" (4 green, 4 yellow, 2 blue, and 2 orange)

From the side B border print, cut:

2 strips, 5" x 38"

3 strips, 5" x 42"

Side A

1. Sew the 2⅞" light and dark triangles together as shown. Make 36.

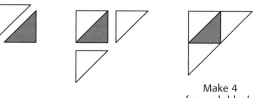

Make 4
for each block.

2. Sew the units from step 1 to the half-square triangles cut from the 4⅞" dark squares.

Make 4
for each block.

3. Assemble the units from step 2, the 1½" x 4½" light rectangles, and the 1½" dark squares as shown to make the Hen and Chicks block. Make 9 blocks.

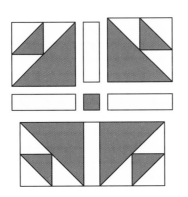

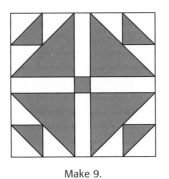

Make 9.

4. Sew the pieces cut from templates A and B together to make the diamond rectangles as shown. Make 12.

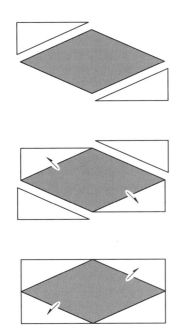

Make 12.

5. Sew the 3⅜" blue-green squares together with the 2½" light triangles to make the square-within-a-square blocks. Make 4.

Make 4.

6. Arrange the blocks, diamond rectangles, and sashing squares on a design wall. Number them as shown and remove.

Side B

1. With the D triangles, make two yellow-and-green triangle squares, one orange-and-yellow triangle square, and one green-and-blue triangle square.

Make 2.   Make 1.   Make 1.

2. Arrange the C triangles, rectangles, and triangle squares for side B on a design wall as shown.

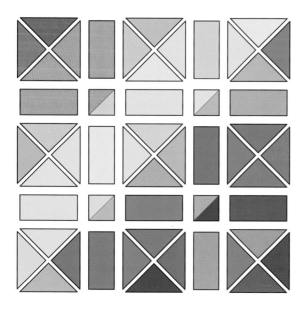

3. When you have them arranged the way you want them, remove just two triangles at a time and sew the triangles of the same color together in pairs—sew two purple triangles together, two red triangles together, two orange triangles, and so on. Place them back on the design wall to keep track of your arrangement. Number the blocks, if desired, beginning at the upper right corner.

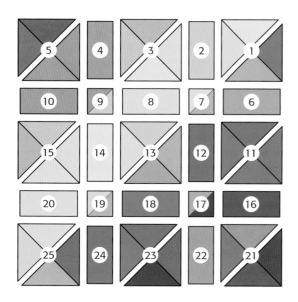

QUILT ASSEMBLY

1. Work with one block at a time. Place Hen and Chicks block 1, right side down, on your work table and place a batting square on top of it.

2. Beginning with the upper right corner, remove the two triangle units for block 1 from the design wall. Place them, right sides together, on top of the batting square. Be sure that you have the triangles oriented in the same direction as they were on the design wall. Arrange the triangles so that the seam will create a diagonal stitching line exactly through the center of the Hen and Chicks block as shown. Pin to secure the triangles.

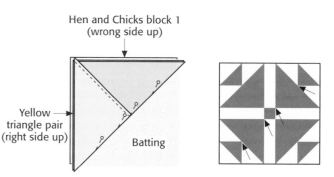

Place pins so they intersect points on the Hen and Chicks block.

3. With invisible thread in your bobbin, sew through all thicknesses and finger-press the seam.

4. Stitch in the ditch on the other seam, making sure you have lined it up so the bobbin threads will intersect the corners of the Hen and Chicks block underneath.

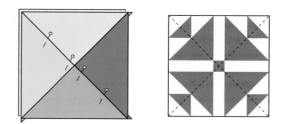

5. From the Hen and Chicks side, trim and square the block to 9½" x 9½" if needed. (There will be very little to trim; you are really just "tidying up" the block.) Return the block to the design wall. Repeat for all nine Hen and Chicks blocks.

6. To join the blocks with wide sashing, remove one rectangle at a time from the design wall, beginning with block 2 from side B. Align one long edge, right sides together, with the triangle side (side B) of block 1. Be sure to keep the block oriented in the correct position. Take the diamond rectangle 2 from side A and turn one long edge under ¼" and press. Align the unfolded long edge, right sides together with the Hen and Chicks side of the block. Sew together. You will be sewing both pieces of sashing to the same block at the same time.

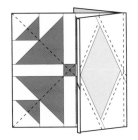

Sew both sashing strips
to the block at the same time.

7. Sew the next block (3) to the other long edge of the side B rectangle. Measure the space between the two seam allowances and cut a piece of batting the same size. It should be about 3½" x 9½". Place the batting rectangle in the space and cover with the diamond rectangle. Hand or machine sew the folded edge down.

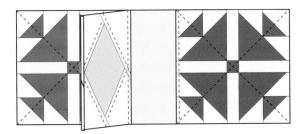

8. Add the next sashing rectangle and block in the same manner to create the top row. Repeat to make three rows.

9. With invisible thread in your bobbin, quilt in the ditch around the diamonds.

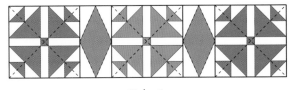

Make 3.

10. Sew two sashing rows for side A, using the diamond rectangles and square-in-a-square units as shown. Sew two sashing rows for side B, using the rectangles and triangle squares as shown.

Make 2 for side A.

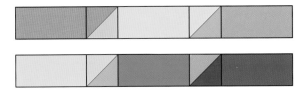

Make 1 each for side B.

11. Press under ¼" along one long edge of the side A sashing row and join the rows together in the same way you joined the blocks together. Quilt in the ditch around the diamonds as you go.

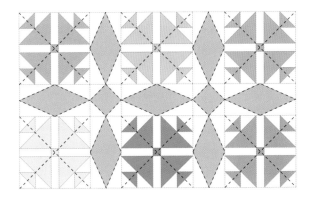

12. Join the three 42"-long blue-green strips for the side A border end to end to make one long strip. Cut two pieces, 5" x 47", for the side borders. Repeat with the side B border strips.

13. Place a 38"-long batting strip between a side A and a side B 38"-long border strip. Pin or spray-baste, and quilt as desired. Make two border strips.

14. Measure your quilt from side to side through the center to determine the length needed for the top and bottom borders. Trim the two quilted borders to 4½" wide by the measured length.

15. Place a 47"-long batting strip between a side A and a side B 47"-long border strip. Pin or spray-baste and quilt as desired. Make two border strips.

16. Measure the quilt from top to bottom through the center and trim the two quilted borders to 4½" wide by the measured length.

17. Referring to "Borders with a Contrasting Inner Border" on page 25, join the top and bottom border strips to the quilt with contrasting sashing strips.

18. Referring to "Pieced Sashing" on page 22, cut and sew a border-fabric rectangle to each end of the sashing strips for the sides. Make two for each side of the quilt. Join the side borders to the quilt with the pieced sashing strips.

19. Referring to "Basic Binding" on page 26 or "Reversible Binding" on page 28, cut strips and bind the edges of the quilt.

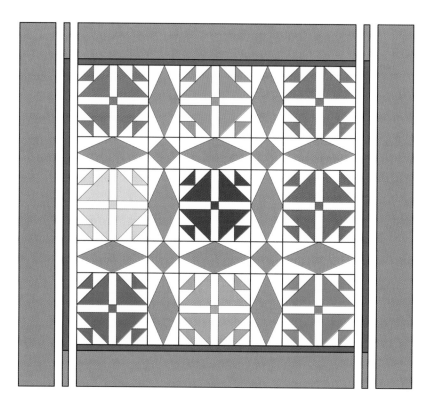

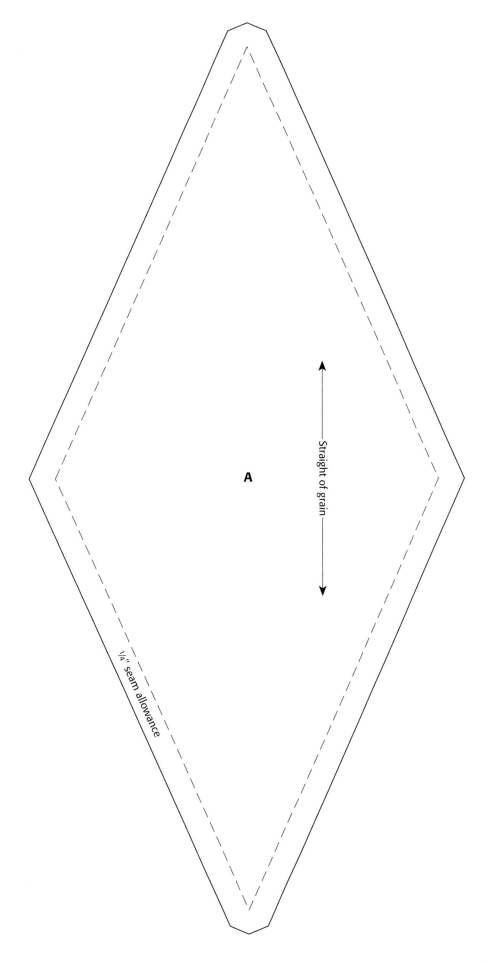

A

Straight of grain

¼" seam allowance

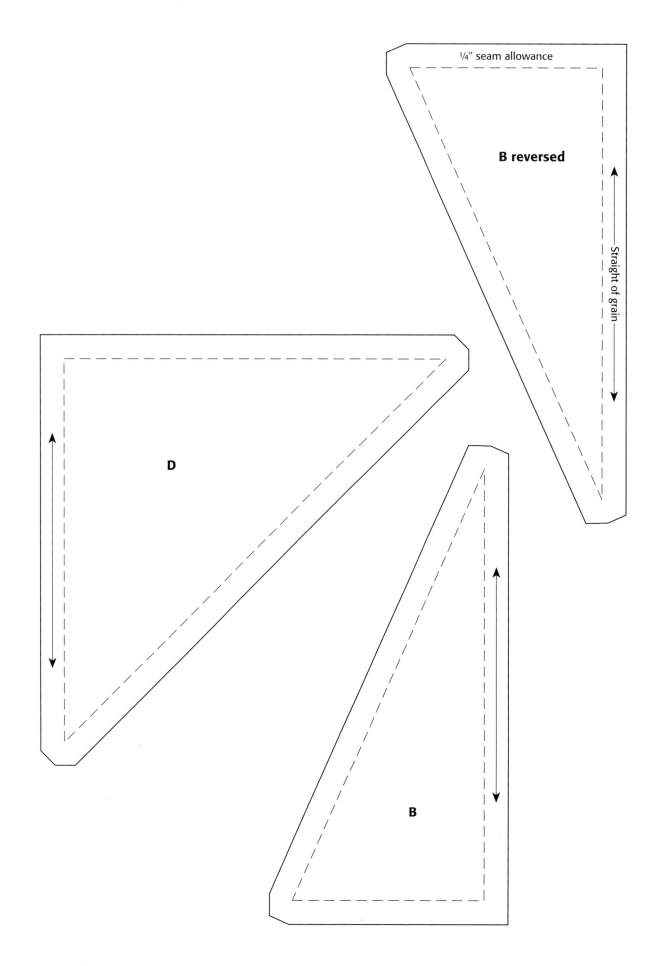

¼" seam allowance

B reversed

Straight of grain

D

B

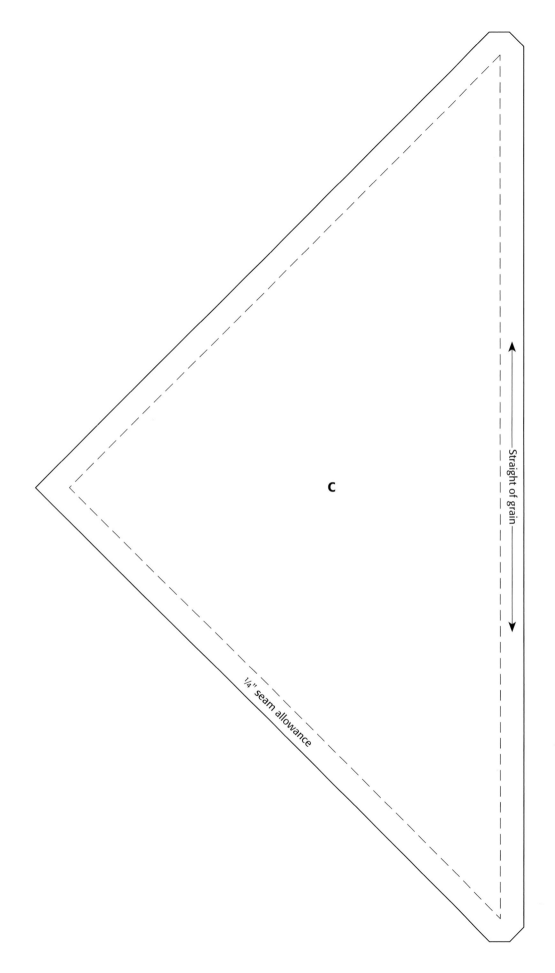

C

Straight of grain

¼" seam allowance

Quilt: 26¼" x 35½"
Made by Sharon Pederson, Ionne McCauley, and Mary Ellen Kranz

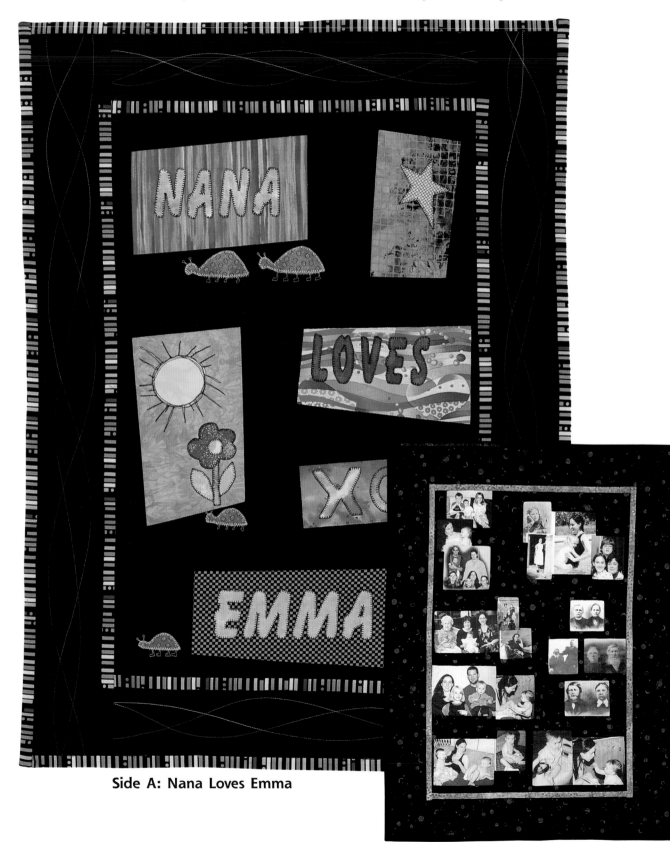

Side A: Nana Loves Emma

Side B: Family Tree

NANA LOVES EMMA

For my newest granddaughter, Emma, I wanted to make a whimsical quilt to tell her I loved her. I also wanted a free-form look without having to sew unusual shapes together. On graph paper, I first drew blocks that would be easy to sew together. Then I fused "wonky" (a highly technical term) blocks onto them. I drew the appliqué images to look as if a child had done them—that's what people who can't draw do to cover up the fact that they can't draw! I fused the appliqué shapes and then blanket stitched them by machine, combining appliqué and quilting steps into one.

The technique used on the other side of the quilt was taught to me by my friend Mary Ellen Kranz, who teaches computer skills to quilters. After a class with Mary Ellen, you can call yourself a *queek*, which is of course a combination of *quilter* and *geek*. See "Resources" on page 94 for further information on her classes.

Mary Ellen is writing a book about the use of photographs on quilts, and I was thrilled when she offered to make a quilt for my book. You can see it on page 55.

MATERIALS

Yardages are based on 42"-wide fabrics.

Side A
- 1⅛ yards of black fabric for background and borders*
- 1 fat quarter *each* of 6 assorted bright prints for wonky rectangles
- Assorted scraps for appliqué
- 1 yard of fusible web

Side B
- 1⅛ yards of dark print for background and borders*
- 7 printable fabric sheets for ink-jet printers, 8½" x 11"**

Basic Sashing*
- ¼ yard for 1⅛"-wide strips
- ⅜ yard for 1¾"-wide strips

Basic Binding
- ⅜ yard

Reversible Binding
- ¼ yard for 1⅛"-wide strips
- ⅜ yard for 1¾"-wide strips

Batting
- ⅝ yard of 96"-wide fusible batting

Note that I used the same fabric as the background for the sashing that joins the blocks on each side. Buy extra background fabric for matching sashing.

**See "Resources" on page 94. See also "Other Photo-Transfer Options" on page 55 if you don't have a computer and scanner.*

CUTTING

From the batting, cut:

1 piece, 10" x 13"

1 piece, 7" x 10"

1 piece, 8" x 12"

1 piece, 7" x 12"

1 piece, 6" x 12"

1 piece, 7" x 19"

2 pieces, 4½" x 20"

2 pieces, 4½" x 38"

From the 6 bright prints, cut:

1 piece, 6" x 9"

1 piece, 5" x 7½"

1 piece, 6" x 10"

1 piece, 5" x 9"

1 piece, 3" x 9"

1 piece, 5" x 10½"

From *each* of the black and dark-print fabrics, cut:

1 piece, 10" x 13"

1 piece, 7" x 10"

1 piece, 8" x 12"

1 piece, 7" x 12"

1 piece, 6" x 12"

1 piece, 7" x 19"

2 pieces, 4½" x 20"

2 pieces, 4½" x 38"

From the fusible web and appliqué fabrics, cut:

1 star, 1 flower, 1 sun, 3 large ladybugs, 2 small ladybugs, Xs and Os, and other letters you need using the patterns on pages 56–57.

SIDE A

1. Use a rotary cutter and ruler to trim the six rectangles cut from the bright prints so they are no longer perfect rectangles—make them look wonky. Trim them so that when they are fused to the black background rectangles, the edges are at least 1" away from any edge of the black background. This is to allow for trimming after the block is quilted.

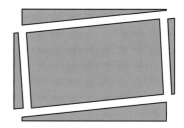

2. Fuse or spray-baste the wonky shapes to each black background piece.

3. With invisible thread, zigzag stitch around the edges.

4. Fuse the appliqué motifs onto each block, following the manufacturer's instructions.

5. Layer each side A block onto its batting piece and fuse. Hold the iron about ⅛" above the fabric when you are fusing so it won't flatten the batting.

6. With black thread in the needle and light-colored thread in the bobbin, blanket stitch around the appliqué pieces or use any of the decorative stitches on your machine. Change the stitch pattern to add other details as you go—add feet and antenna to the ladybugs, and rays around the sun. You will be quilting without a backing fabric.

For Softer Appliqués

To avoid stiffness, use just a narrow strip of fusible web around the edges when fusing large pieces. Be sure the fusible web goes out to the edges to avoid the shaggy appliqué look.

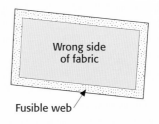

Wrong side of fabric

Fusible web

Side B

1. The fun part of this quilt is collecting the pictures. Once you have decided which ones to include, scan them into your computer. If you have a digital camera, you can also take new pictures and download them from your camera into your computer. If you don't have a computer, see "Other Photo-Transfer Options" on page 55.

2. Once in the computer, use photo management software to arrange them in groups that will fit within the dimensions of your blocks. You can leave spaces around each one or overlap them if you prefer.

3. With an ink-jet printer, print them onto fabric sheets, following the manufacturer's instructions.

4. Now you can treat the photo-fabric sheets like any other piece of fabric. They can be ironed, appliquéd, reverse appliquéd, or pieced into blocks. For this quilt, I used reverse appliqué to cover up as much of the white fabric sheet as possible. I wanted the look of a bulletin board or scrapbook with lots of pictures arranged randomly. Appliqué a group of photos to each of the dark-print background pieces.

Making Templates for Reverse Appliqué

1. To make a template for reverse appliqué, place the fabric with photo images, right side down, on a light box and cover with a piece of freezer paper, shiny side down.

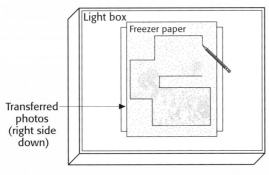

Trace around image.

2. Trace around each photo onto the dull side of the freezer paper and then cut on the drawn lines.

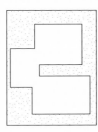

Cut on drawn lines and remove.

3. Iron the freezer-paper template onto the wrong side of your background fabric.

4. Trim the excess fabric away, leaving between 1/8" and 1/4" seam allowance. Turn the seam allowance under and press or glue in place with fabric glue.

Fabric (wrong side up)

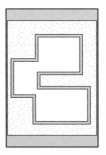

Trim fabric, leaving 1/4" seam allowance.

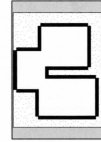

Turn seam allowance under.

5. Place on top of your photo images, pin in place, and appliqué. I use a very narrow zigzag stitch. Then gently remove the freezer paper.

Place fabric with "window" over transferred photos and appliqué in place.

5. Layer the side B pieces and the side A pieces together with the batting and fuse. Trim the Nana block to 9½" x 12½", the Star block to 6½" x 9½", the Flower block to 7½' x 11½", the Loves block to 6½" x 11½", the XOX block to 5½" x 11½", and the Emma block to 6½" x 18½".

QUILT ASSEMBLY

1. Arrange the blocks for side A as shown. Referring to "Basic Sashing" on page 21, join the blocks and rows together. After joining the Nana and the Star blocks for row 1, and the Flower block, the Loves block and the XOX blocks for row 2, do any additional trimming necessary to make them the same width. Similarly, after joining the Loves block and the XOX blocks, you might have to do some trimming to make them the same height as the Flower block. This is where the extra 1" of black background comes in handy.

2. Place a 20"-long batting strip between a 20"-long side A and side B border strip. Fuse and quilt as desired. Make two border strips. Measure the width of your quilt through the middle. Trim the strips to 4" wide and the determined length.

3. Repeat step 2 for the 38"-long border strips. Trim to 4" wide.

4. Referring to "Borders with a Contrasting Inner Border" on page 25, join the top and bottom border strips to the quilt with contrasting sashing strips.

5. Referring to "Pieced Sashing" on page 22, sew a border-fabric rectangle to each end of the sashing strips for the sides. Make two for side A and two for side B. Measure the length of the quilt and trim the side borders to the correct length. Join the side borders to the quilt with the pieced sashing strips.

6. Referring to "Basic Binding" on page 26 or "Reversible Binding" on page 28, cut strips and bind the edges of the quilt.

Sharon's Suggestion

If you want a different font for the letters needed to write your version of "Nana Loves Emma," use your computer. Type your sentiment and then choose a font that you like for your quilt. Enlarge the text until it is the size you want, approximately 2¼" high for uppercase letters. Then instruct the computer to print the text mirror-imaged so the letters will be going the right way for the fusible-appliqué technique.

Other Photo-Transfer Options

There are several ways to transfer photos to fabric and several books available to help you (see "Resources" on page 94). If you don't have access to a computer, scanner, or digital camera, the simplest way is to use photo-transfer paper for color copiers.

Once you have chosen your photographs, arrange them in groupings to fit the rectangles for the quilt. You might want to tape them onto a regular sheet of paper to keep them in place. You may find that you need to reduce or enlarge some of them first. Find a reliable copy center where you can get assistance if you need it. Use a laser color photocopier to copy the photographs onto the 8½" x 11" photo-transfer paper. Follow the manu-facturer's instructions and be sure to mirror-image the photos when copying so that your family and friends are not backwards on your quilt.

When the photos are copied onto the transfer paper, you will need to heat-set them onto your fabric with an iron or heat press. Some quilt shops have a heat press that you can use for a fee, and I have also gone to a company that makes custom-designed T-shirts.

Once the design is transferred onto fabric, you're good to go. Begin at step 4 of side B on page 53.

Beach Cottage Windows by Mary Ellen Kranz.

Each side of this delightful quilt features a single photo; one shows the view from the front window of a cottage, and the other shows the view from the back. My friend Mary Ellen enlarged each photo in sections and printed the sections onto fabric sheets using her inkjet printer. She then stitched the segments together with sashing and borders so that the finished quilt looks like a scene being viewed through a paned window. This is one of the techniques she teaches in her Computer Skills for Quilters class.

Appliqué Patterns

Patterns are reversed for fusible appliqué.

Embroidery placement

Quilt: 29" x 29"
Made by Ionne McCauley

Side A: Clouds

Side B: Energy Radiated—Energy Contained

ALL-DAY SUCKER

am not an art quilter, but I hang out with a lot of people who are. I love their ability to work without the safety net of a pattern, but I would probably break out in hives if I tried to do it. I know that providing a pattern for an art quilt is an oxymoron, but I really wanted to include a piece you could call an art quilt in this book. Ionne McCauley and I put our heads together and came up with the "All-Day Sucker." The spiral reminds me of suckers we used to get when we were kids, and it took Ionne all day to make it. Do you remember lying on your back watching clouds float by? That's what the other side reminds me of. So here we have two of my favorite childhood memories rolled into one.

We had lots of fun making this; Ionne drew the spiral because I was once told by a teacher that I was "spirally challenged." Good thing he was smiling when he said it.

My intention is to give you an idea as a springboard, not specific pattern pieces. Now it's up to you to create your own art quilt. By the way, Ionne made this one, with only technical advice from me.

MATERIALS

Yardages are based on 42"-wide fabrics.

Side A
- 1½ yards total of assorted batiks and hand-dyed fabrics

Side B
- 1 yard total of assorted hand-dyed fabrics and subtle prints of various widths and lengths*
- 1 square, 22" x 22", red batik for spiral
- 1 square, 22" x 22", green batik for spiral

Basic Binding
- ⅜ yard

Reversible Binding
- ¼ yard for 1⅛"-wide strips
- ⅜ yard for 1¾"-wide strips

Batting and Supplies
- ¾ yard of 96"-wide fusible batting
- 1 yard of fusible web
- Freezer paper
- Compass for drawing circles with a 9½" radius

The pieces range from 1¼" to 3½" wide and from 5" to 13" long.

SIDE A

1. Cut two pieces of freezer paper, each 14½" x 29". Find the center of the long side and draw a vertical line to divide the paper into two equal squares. Set the compass point on the midpoint at the edge of the paper, and with a radius of 9½", draw a quarter circle on each square. Carefully cut each piece in half and cut the circle pieces out. You will use all eight pieces as templates. Set the corner pieces aside.

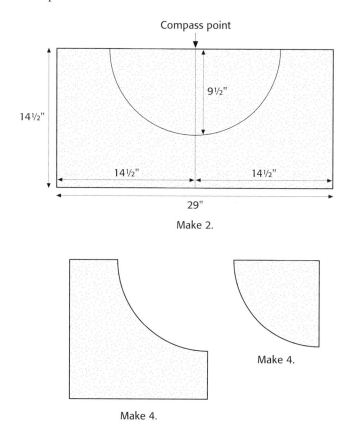

Make 2.

Make 4.

Make 4.

2. Refer to the photograph of side A on page 58 and study the quarter circles. Ionne used a combination of piecing and raw-edge appliqué to create those sections. She pieced strips randomly and then machine appliquéd curved shapes onto them, as shown above right. Using whatever techniques you prefer, piece four sections a little larger than the quarter circles. You might want to sketch designs right onto the freezer paper and use that as a guide.

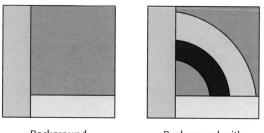

Background   Background with Appliquéd Arcs

Piecing Options

3. Iron the freezer paper onto the wrong side of the four pieced sections you have just made and trim the straight sides, leaving ¼" for seam allowance. You can trim some of the excess fabric around the outer edge if needed, but leave plenty of extra.

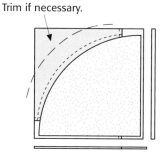

Trim if necessary.

Trim straight edges only, leaving a ¼" seam allowance.

4. Sew the four sections together to make a circle.

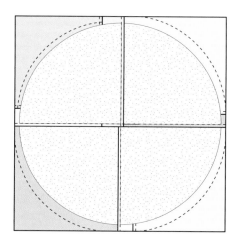

5. Refer to the photograph of side A and study the corner sections. In a similar manner, randomly piece four corner sections, using the freezer-paper templates as guides. Make the pieces about ½" larger than the templates all around. Set aside.

SIDE B

1. On a 22" square of freezer paper, draw a 19" circle and a spiral within it. You will have to tape two pieces together because freezer paper is only 18" wide.

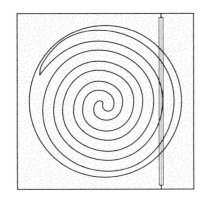

2. Layer your two spiral fabrics right sides up and iron the freezer-paper template onto the top piece. Pin the three layers together.

3. With a short stitch and thread that matches the top fabric, stitch on the spiral lines and the outside circle line. Remove half of the freezer paper, leaving one spiral as a guide. This is so you won't get lost in the spiral and accidentally cut away something you shouldn't.

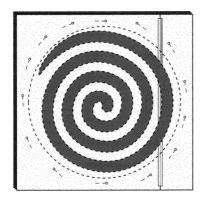

Sharon's Suggestion
The close stitching will perforate the freezer paper to make removal fairly easy. If you have any trouble removing it, carefully insert a seam ripper to get it started.

4. Cutting close to the stitching line, cut the top fabric away from the section with no freezer paper. After you have finished cutting, you can remove the remaining freezer paper from the spiral, but leave it pinned to the area outside the circle for stability.

5. With decorative thread, satin stitch around all edges of the spiral. Do not stitch around the outer edge of the circle.

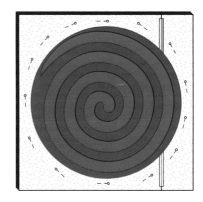

QUILT ASSEMBLY

1. Draw a circle with a radius of 9½" onto freezer paper to use as a guide to cut a 19" circle from the fusible batting. Center the side A circle on the batting circle and trim the fabric edges even with the batting. Center the side B spiral on the other side. Remove the freezer paper from side B and trim the spiral even with the batting. Fuse the three layers together.

2. With decorative thread in your needle and black thread in your bobbin, quilt from the spiral side in random circles or follow the spiral design.

3. Use a freezer-paper template for the corner sections as a pattern to cut four pieces of fusible batting. Fuse a side A corner piece to each one.

4. Starting in the corner of the fused batting, place a wedge-shaped strip right side up. Place a second piece on top, with right sides together. Sew with a ¼" seam. Remember your bobbin thread will show on side A, so choose something decorative or invisible.

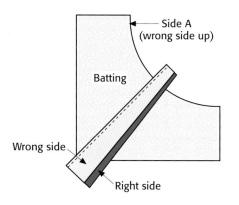

5. Carefully iron the pieces open by touching very gently with the tip of the iron. Or, finger press the seam and then hold the iron ⅛" above it.

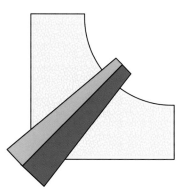

6. Continue adding wedge-shaped pieces until the batting is covered. Make four.

7. Trim only the inner straight sides of the corner sections even with the batting.

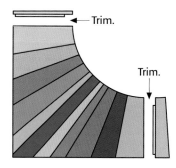

8. Arrange the four corner sections as shown; butt the edges together.

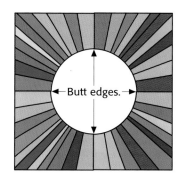

9. Cut four sashing pieces, each 1" x 5½", to join the four corners of side A. If you don't want the sashing to be noticeable, cut the pieces from fabrics that will match or blend with the areas they will join. Attach fusible web to the wrong side of each piece and center one piece over each of the butted edges. Fuse the four sections together with the sashing. Repeat on side B. With matching thread in your needle and invisible thread in the bobbin, sew both edges of the sashing strip with a wide zigzag stitch.

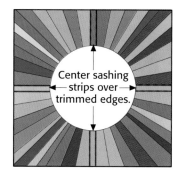

Side B

10. Using the same freezer-paper guide you used to cut the batting and trim the 19" circles, center it on the four corner sections and iron it in place along the edges. Using the edge of the freezer-paper circle as your guide, draw a line on the quilt top. Remove the freezer paper and trim right on the line. The circle portion will then fit exactly into this opening.

11. On a large, flat pressing surface, put the circle piece into the circular opening. You may have to put a towel on your cutting table so that your quilt will lie completely flat. A standard ironing board is probably too narrow.

12. To create sashing for joining the circle to the corners, draw a circle onto the paper backing of fusible web, using the 19" circle of freezer paper. You may need to "piece" the fusible web together, or you could fold the freezer paper in half and draw two half circles. Draw another line ½" on either side of the circle. Cut on the outside lines. Make two.

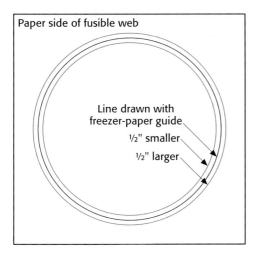

Paper side of fusible web

Line drawn with freezer-paper guide

½" smaller

½" larger

Cut on red lines.

13. It isn't necessary to do your sashing in a continuous circle. You can cut it into quarters to make it easier. This would also allow you to use four different fabrics if you want.

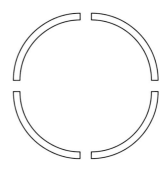

14. Pin the fusible-web arcs to the wrong side of your sashing fabrics and cut out. Working on one side at a time, center the sashing pieces over the edge of the circle and fuse them. After you have fused both sides, quilt over the lines with decorative or invisible thread.

Note: Our side A was not done this way; it was zigzag stitched to hold the pieces in place. Using sashing on both sides is a more secure alternative.

15. Referring to "Basic Binding" on page 26 or "Reversible Binding" on page 28, cut strips and bind the edges of the quilt.

Quilt: 36" x 54" • Finished block: 8½" x 8½"
Made by Sharon Pederson and Ionne McCauley

Side A: My Side

Side B: My Mom's Side

KEEPING PEACE IN THE FAMILY

*W*hen I went to school, most of the kids had one Mom and one Dad and assorted sisters and brothers—sometimes a lot of them. Now there are many variations on the theme of family, and new etiquette is often required. When I asked a new friend how many grandchildren she had, she replied, "Three homegrown, and two that came with their mothers." I loved her way of including all of the kids into her circle of love while managing to indicate the way they arrived.

One of the newly arrived grandchildren was a young teenage girl, and my friend asked her what color she would like her quilt to be. All of her other grandchildren had quilts, of course, and this one would, too. The girl said purple and yellow and not old-fashioned looking; her mother said pink and traditional. As you can imagine, my friend wanted to please both her new granddaughter and her new daughter-in-law, but she didn't want to make two quilts. So, I suggested an alternative. Why not make it reversible and whoever made the bed could choose which side was up. I hope this helps keep peace in the family.

MATERIALS

Yardages are based on 42"-wide fabrics.

Side A
- 1⅜ yards total of assorted purple fabrics for blocks
- 1⅜ yards total of assorted yellow fabrics for blocks

Side B
- 1½ yards total of assorted fabrics for strips
- 1 yard of floral print for triangles

Basic Sashing
- ⅜ yard for 1⅛"-wide strips
- ⅝ yard for 1¾"-wide strips

Basic Binding
- ½ yard

Reversible Binding
- ¼ yard for 1⅛"-wide strips
- ⅜ yard for 1¾"-wide strips

Batting
- ¾ yard of 96"-wide batting

CUTTING

From the batting, cut:
24 squares, 9" x 9"

From the assorted yellow and purple fabrics, cut:
12 purple squares and 12 yellow squares, each 10¼" x 10¼"

From the floral print, cut:
12 squares, 9⅜" x 9⅜"; cut once diagonally to yield 24 triangles

From the assorted fabrics for side B strips, cut:
Narrow, medium, and wide strips as needed

SIDE A

1. Place one purple square on top of a yellow square, both right sides up. With a rotary cutter, using a gentle curve, cut a random wavy strip out of the middle of each square.

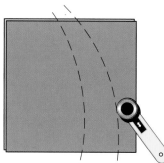

Randomly cut through
both squares.

2. Separate the two colors and switch the middle piece so that there is a yellow strip in the middle of the purple square and vice versa.

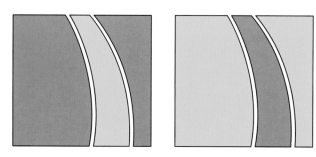

3. Pin, if desired, and sew the pieces together with a ¼"-wide seam allowance. Press the seam toward the darker fabric and trim the blocks to 9" x 9".

4. Referring to the quilt diagram, arrange the blocks on a design wall. Starting at the upper left, number the blocks from 1 to 24.

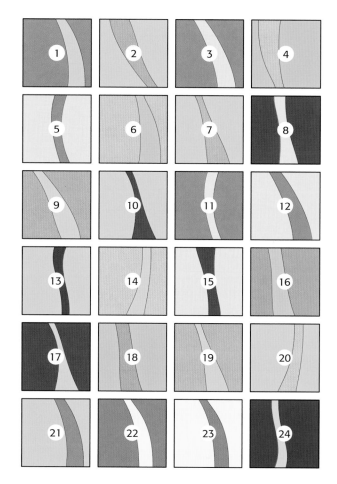

Sharon's Suggestion

When numbering blocks, I write the number on masking tape and stick it on each block on the design wall. If there is a top or bottom, I add an arrow to indicate the top.

Side B

1. Make a sketch for side B. Starting in the upper right, number the blocks from 1 to 24. (Starting in the opposite corner ensures that the numbers on the front and back will correspond to each other.)

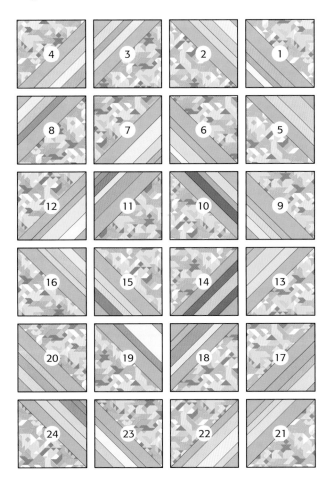

2. Working on one block at a time, place block 1 from side A, right side down, on your work surface and cover with a batting square.

3. Place a floral print triangle, right side up, on the batting, referring to your sketch. Add strips as for the basic block (see page 13 for details if needed). Make 24 blocks, keeping the diagonal line in the middle of the block going the correct way for each block.

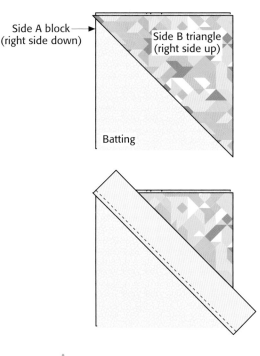

Quilt Assembly

1. Referring to your sketch and to "Basic Sashing" on page 21, join the blocks and rows together.

2. Referring to "Basic Binding" on page 26 or "Reversible Binding" on page 28, cut strips and bind the edges of the quilt.

Quilt: 23" x 28" • Finished hexagon: 7¼" x 8½"
Made by Sharon Pederson and Joanne Corfield

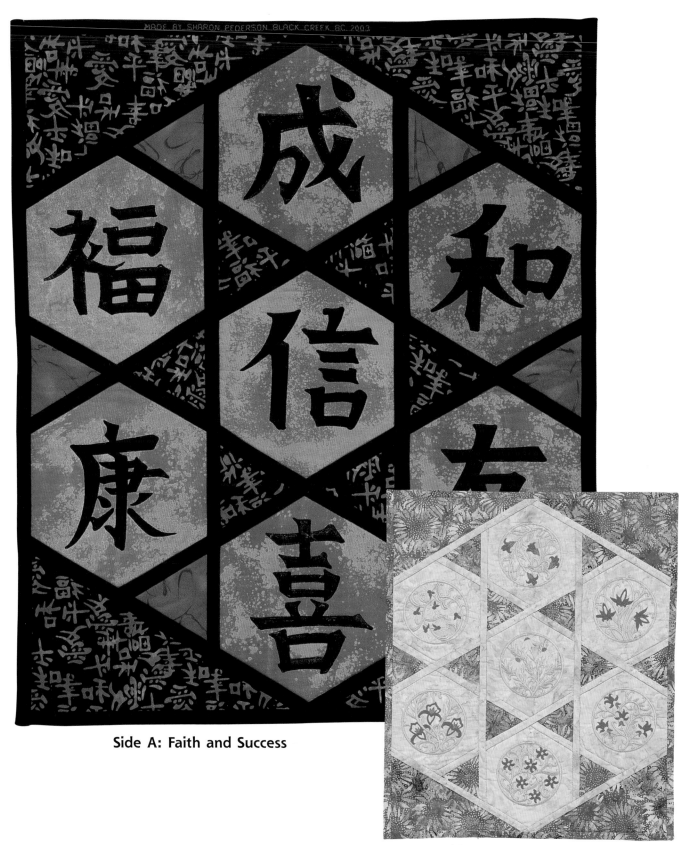

Side A: Faith and Success

Side B: Luck and Friends

68

PEACE, HEALTH, AND HAPPINESS

n the photo gallery of my first book, I included a quilt that used hexagon blocks with machine-appliquéd Japanese Family Crest patterns on them. Since then, I have had many requests for instructions for that quilt, so here they are. I used some wonderful kanji patterns from Indonesian Batiks (see "Resources" on page 94), but you could use any design—printed or appliquéd. The kanji designs I chose translate into the words: peace, health, happiness, faith, success, friend, and luck.

Someone once asked me what feature I would like to see added to sewing machines. My first response was, "Have it serve lattes!" Little did I know that there would soon be an improvement that I would enjoy more than a latte: a sewing machine that also embroiders. As if we didn't have enough choices, now we have access to thousands of beautiful designs that can be embroidered by your machine. My first question when I got my new Bernina 200 was how can I incorporate machine embroidery in a reversible quilt?

If you don't have a machine that does embroidery, consider making this quilt with appliquéd designs on side B. You could also purchase batik art panels in another color, pattern, or theme to use on side B. And of course, hand embroidery would be lovely.

MATERIALS
Yardages are based on 42"-wide fabrics.

Side A
- ½ yard of print fabric for setting and corner triangles
- ¼ yard of solid fabric for setting triangles
- 7 kanji batik art panels or similar fabrics, 8¼" x 9½" (See "Choosing Motifs" on page 70.)

Side B
- 1 yard of background fabric on which to embroider 7 motifs. (This allows for the extra fabric needed to fit into the embroidery hoop on your machine.)
- ½ yard of fabric for setting and corner triangles

Basic Sashing
- ¼ yard for 1⅛"-wide strips
- ⅓ yard for 1¾"-wide strips

Basic Binding
- ¼ yard

Reversible Binding
- ⅛ yard for 1⅛"-wide strips
- ¼ yard for 1¾"-wide strips

Batting and Supplies

◆ ⅝ yard of 96"-wide fusible batting

◆ Compass for drawing circles with a 4½" radius

◆ 10" square of transparent template plastic or cardboard

Machine Embroidery

◆ Embroidery design/pattern, approximately 5¼" diameter (See "Choosing Motifs" below.)

◆ Embroidery threads

◆ Embroidery hoop for your sewing machine

Choosing Motifs

See "Resources" on page 94 for sources of preprinted fabrics and embroidery designs. I used FM 706, FM 752, FM 756, FM 759, FM 761, FM 768, and FM 770 from Oklahoma Embroidery Supply and Design, Inc. (www.oesd.com).

If you choose to do appliqué or hand embroidery instead of buying kanji panels and embroidering by machine, you will need ⅝ yard of background fabric for each side of your quilt.

CUTTING

From the batting, cut:

7 rectangles, 8¼" x 9½"

2 rectangles, 7½" x 12½"; cut once diagonally to yield 4 corner triangles

1 strip, 4½" x 35"

From *each* of the fabrics for setting triangles, cut:

1 strip, 4½" x 35"

From *each* of the fabrics for corner triangles, cut:

2 rectangles, 7½" x 12½"; place right sides together and cut once diagonally to yield 4 triangles

Cutting the Setting Triangles

Cut each of the 4½" x 35" strips of batting and fabric into 12 triangles, using the 60° mark on your ruler, or if you prefer, use template A on page 73.

If you are using two different fabrics for the setting triangles as I did on side A, cut six each of the two fabrics.

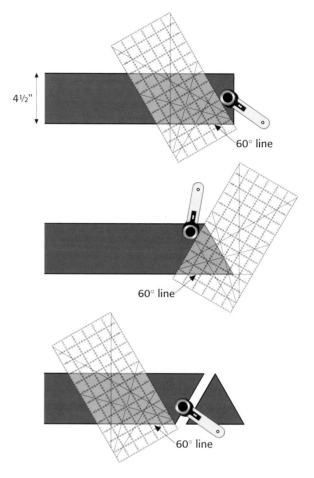

MAKING HEXAGON WINDOW TEMPLATES

1. To draw a hexagon that is 9" from top to bottom, set your compass at 4½" (the radius) and draw a circle on template plastic or cardboard.

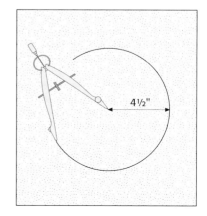

2. Move the point of the compass to the point on the circle that is directly above the center.

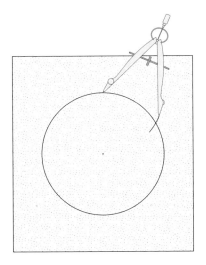

3. Without changing the compass, mark the circle and move the compass point to that mark and mark the circle again. Connect the two points to make the first side of your hexagon.

4. Continue to mark around the circle and connect the marks until you have six sides.

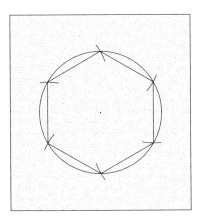

5. Cut out the hexagon and use the window template when centering the motifs.

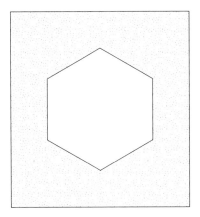

SIDE A

1. Adhere one 8¼" x 9½" rectangle of fusible batting to the wrong side of a kanji batik panel. To do this, hold the iron about ⅛" above the pieces and let the steam fuse the batting so you won't flatten it.

2. With light-colored thread in your bobbin and black thread in your needle, quilt around the design. You won't have a backing fabric underneath since you will fuse a machine-embroidered piece to the batting when the quilting is done. Repeat for all seven blocks.

3. Using your hexagon window template, center the kanji characters in the middle of the window. Mark the cutting line by tracing inside the template window. Trim the panel on the lines.

4. Layer a batting triangle between a side A and a side B setting triangle and fuse. Repeat for all 12 setting triangles.

5. Layer a batting triangle between a side A and a side B corner triangle and fuse. Repeat for all four corner triangles. Quilt as desired.

Note: The hexagon blocks are quilted around the kanji characters, and the setting triangles are small enough to leave unquilted if desired. However, the corner triangles need some quilting to hold the batting in place. The manufacturer's recommendation for Hobbs Fusible Batting is to quilt every 4".

SIDE B

1. Embroider or appliqué seven designs onto your background fabric. Using the hexagon window template, mark the cutting lines, making sure you center the motif in the template window. Cut along the marked lines.

2. Fuse to the batting on the reverse side of the seven kanji character blocks. Be sure that both sides are going in the correct direction.

QUILT ASSEMBLY

1. Arrange the blocks, setting triangles, and corner triangles on your design wall.

2. Referring to "Basic Sashing" on page 21, join the blocks and rows together as shown.

Note: The setting and corner triangles are larger than necessary so they will have to be trimmed after they are sewn in place. When joining the setting triangles to the hexagon blocks, center the triangle on the side of the hexagon, and when sewn in place, trim the excess off.

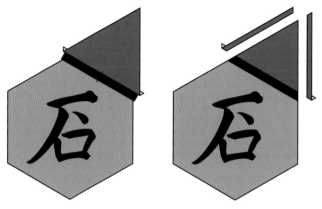

Center the triangle.   Trim.

Trim.

3. Referring to "Basic Binding" on page 26 or "Reversible Binding" on page 28, cut strips and bind the edges of the quilt.

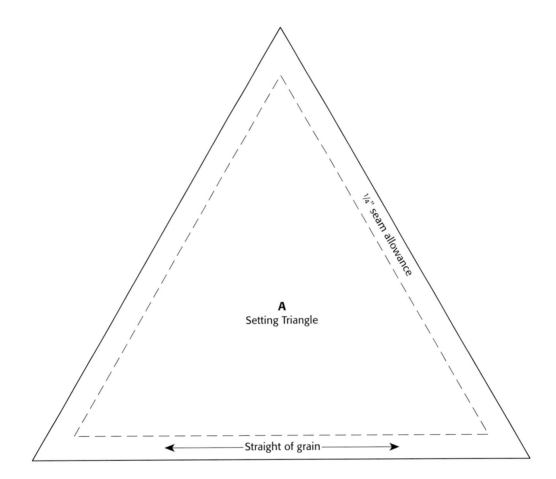

A
Setting Triangle

¼" seam allowance

Straight of grain

Quilt: 48" x 48" • Finished block: 11½" x 11½"
Made by Sharron Evans

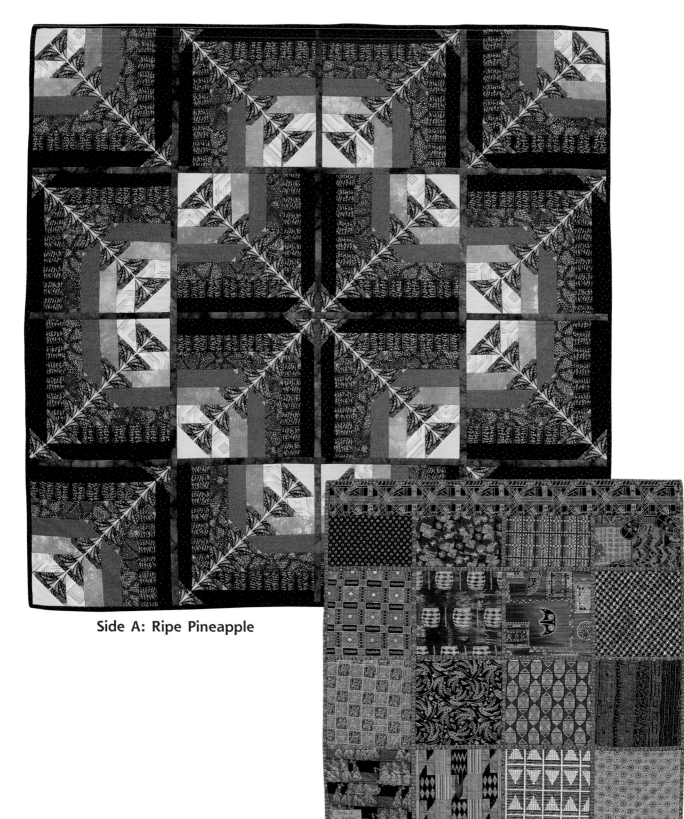

Side A: Ripe Pineapple

Side B: African Prints

Log Cabin by the Lake

I met Sharron Evans in the summer of 2002 while teaching at Quilting-by-the-Lake in Morrisville, New York. Sharron had signed up for all five days with me, and I knew she wasn't your average quilter when I overheard her talking with another student about the 1,000 jumps she had made out of airplanes. Her block wasn't typical either—it was larger than the size I recommended in the supply list. (Now I ask you, is a woman who jumps out of airplanes going to follow directions?) But, students, like customers, are always right, so I just kept a close eye on how she was doing. I have to tell you, the first block wasn't anything to write home about, but by the time she had four done I was very excited about her quilt. I'm sure you will agree.

On the reverse side of Sharron's pieced block, she used some of her stash of exciting African print fabrics. This gives you two very different looks. The African side gives you plenty of opportunity to embellish to your heart's content.

Sharron subsequently went on to solve the problem of attaching a hanging sleeve to a reversible quilt. Her solution is on page 30.

MATERIALS

Yardages are based on 42"-wide fabrics.

Side A

- ¾ yard of novelty print or accent fabric for triangles*
- ¼ yard of yellow solid for strips
- ¼ yard of yellow print for strips
- ⅜ yard of orange fabric for strips
- ½ yard of red fabric for strips
- ½ yard of black-green-and-red print for strips
- ⅝ yard of green print for strips
- ¾ yard of black print for strips

Side B

- 2⅜ yards total of assorted African prints
- Beads and buttons for embellishment (optional)

Basic Sashing

- ⅜ yard for 1⅛"-wide strips
- ½ yard for 1¾"-wide strips

Basic Binding

- ⅝ yard

Reversible Binding

- ⅜ yard for 1⅛"-wide strips
- ½ yard for 1¾"-wide strips

Batting

- 1¼ yards of 96"-wide batting

*Purchase extra fabric if you want to fussy cut your triangles.

Cutting

From the batting cut:
16 squares, 12½" x 12½"

From the African prints, cut:
16 squares, 12½" x 12½"

From the novelty print, cut:
112 A triangles (see template pattern on page 77)
    OR 56 squares, 3¾" x 3¾"; cut once diagonally
    to yield 112 triangles

From the yellow solid, cut:
8 squares, 3¾" x 3¾"; cut once diagonally to
    yield 16 triangles

From the yellow print, cut:
32 strips, 2" x 3½"

From the orange fabric, cut:
32 strips, 2" x 5"

From the red fabric, cut:
32 strips, 2" x 6½"

From the black/green/red print, cut:
32 strips, 2" x 8"

From the green print, cut:
32 strips, 2" x 9½"

From the black print, cut:
32 strips, 2" x 11"

Block Assembly

1. Place one African-print square, right side
   down, on your work surface and cover with a
   batting square.

2. Place one yellow solid triangle, right side up,
   and a novelty fabric triangle, right side down,

on a corner of a batting square. Sew through
all thicknesses with a ¼" seam; flip open and
finger-press.

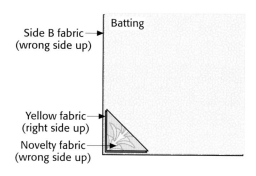

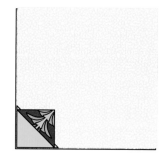

3. Place a 2" x 3½" yellow print strip, right side
   down, on one side of the square; sew, flip,
   and finger-press.

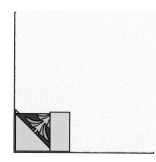

4. Place another 2" x 3½" yellow strip on the
   other side; sew, flip, and finger-press.

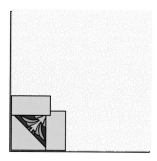

5. Draw a line on the yellow fabric, ¼" beyond the corner of the square; place a novelty fabric triangle, right side down, aligning the long edge of the triangle with the pencil line. Sew, trim the excess yellow fabric, flip and finger-press.

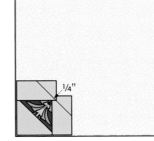

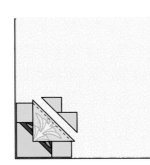

Trim excess.

6. Continue in this fashion with the orange fabric, red fabric, black/red/green print, green print, and black print.

7. Align the diagonal line on a 12½" square ruler with the triangle points and trim the block to 12" x 12". Be sure to allow ¼" for seam allowances beyond the triangle points at the solid yellow corner.

Quilt Assembly

1. Arrange the blocks on a design wall as shown.

2. Referring to "Basic Sashing" on page 21, cut sashing strips for sides A and B. Join the blocks and rows with sashing strips.

3. Referring to "Basic Binding" on page 26 or "Reversible Binding" on page 28, cut strips and bind the edges of the quilt.

4. Embellish side B with beads and buttons as desired.

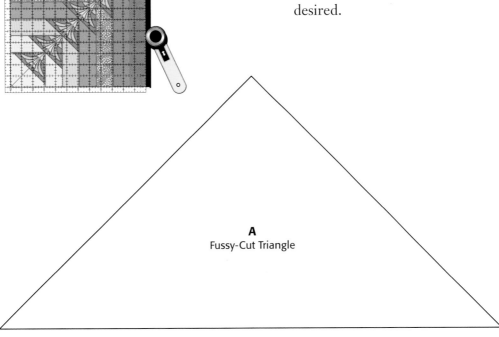

A
Fussy-Cut Triangle

Quilt: 47" x 47" • Finished block: 9" x 9"
Made by Sharon Pederson and Ionne McCauley

Side A: Jean's Star

Side B: Hornby's Twilight

JEAN'S STAR

*O*ccasionally, when teaching, you get students who are so creative you can just sit back and watch them run with the technique. In Morrisville, New York, in the summer of 2002, I had such a class. There are two quilts in this book that came out of that class.

Jean Biddick was one of those very creative students. All I did was show her how to put the blocks together and she came up with this delightful star. I asked her then if I could use her design in a future book and she graciously agreed.

On the other side, I have re-created a quilt I made many years ago in collaboration with my friend Lynne Lovegrove for a mutual friend's first baby. I loved it then and wasn't quite ready to say good-bye to it when we had to send it off. I have often thought of it and knew someday I would make one for myself. The cat in the quilt is Hornby, who arrived on our doorstep 17 years ago. She now spends most of her time on the windowsill (over the baseboard heater), dreaming about the days she used to go out and terrorize the birds.

MATERIALS

Yardages are based on 42"-wide fabrics.

Side A
- 1⅝ yards total of assorted blue fabrics for blocks and 1⅛"-wide sashing
- ⅞ yard of blue print for borders
- ⅞ yard total of assorted orange fabrics for blocks and 1⅛"-wide sashing
- ¾ yard total of assorted yellow fabrics for blocks and 1⅛"-wide sashing

Side B
- 1⅞ yards total of assorted lights, darks, and floral colorwash-type fabrics for blocks
- ¾ yard of brown "wood grain" print for 1¾"-wide sashing strips

- ⅝ yard *each* of light and dark blue fabric for borders*
- 1 fat quarter of black fabric for cat

Basic Binding
- ½ yard

Reversible Binding
- ¼ yard for 1⅛"-wide strips
- ⅜ yard for 1¾"-wide strips

Batting
- 1 yard of 96"-wide batting

*If you want the binding to match the two different borders as in the quilt in the photograph, you will need ⅞ yard each of the two blue fabrics.

CUTTING

From the batting cut:

16 squares, 10" x 10"

4 strips, 5" x 39"

4 squares, 5" x 5"

From the assorted orange fabrics, cut:

8 squares, 5½" x 5½"; cut once diagonally to yield 16 triangles

2 strips, 1⅛" x 42"

Narrow, medium, and wide strips as needed

From the assorted blue fabrics, cut:

4 squares, 5" x 5"

12 squares, 5½" x 5½"; cut once diagonally to yield 24 triangles

4 strips, 1⅛" x 42"

Narrow, medium, and wide strips as needed

From the colorwash fabrics for side B, cut:

144 squares, 3¾" x 3¾"

From the assorted yellow fabrics, cut:

3 strips, 1⅛" x 42"

Narrow, medium, and wide strips as needed

From the brown "wood grain" print, cut:

11 strips, 1¾" x 42"

From the blue border print for side A, cut:

4 strips, 5" x 39"

4 squares, 5" x 5"

From *each* of the light and dark blue border fabrics for side B, cut:

2 strips, 5" x 39"

2 squares, 5½" x 5½"; cut once diagonally to yield 4 triangles

SIDE A

1. Sew two orange triangles to each 5" blue square.

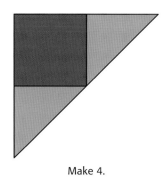

Make 4.

2. Sew eight orange triangles to eight blue triangles to make eight triangle squares.

Make 8.

3. To each triangle square sew two blue triangles; make four with the orange triangle on the left and four with the orange triangle on the right.

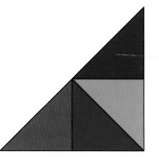

Make 4.

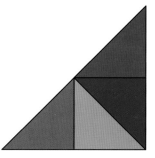

Make 4.

Side B

1. Referring to the color photo of side B on page 78, arrange the 3¾" squares into 16 Nine Patch blocks on a design wall. Keep track of your layout and trim the B patches to 3½" x 3¾"; trim the C patch to 3½" x 3½".

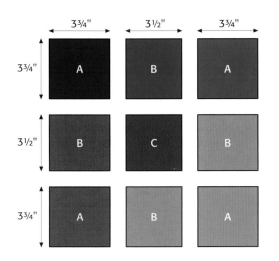

2. Sew the patches together in three rows of three, using a ¼" seam allowance. Press the seams in alternate directions as shown. Sew the three rows together. Press toward the center row and return the blocks to the design wall.

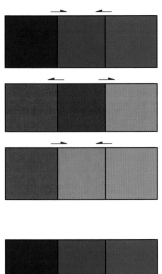

3. Number the blocks from 1 to 16, starting in the upper right-hand corner.

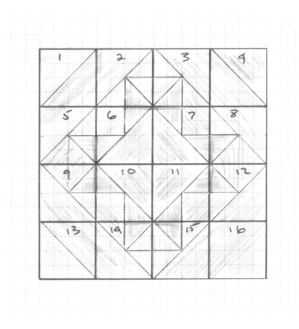

4. To blocks 10 and 11, appliqué flowers from the floral prints, using your favorite method of appliqué. Refer to the photo of side B on page 78.

Block Assembly

1. Make a colored sketch of side A. Starting in the upper left-hand corner, number the blocks from 1 to 16.

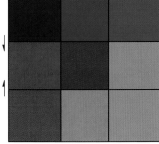

2. Working on one block at a time, place block 1 from side B, right side down, on your work surface and cover with a 10" batting square.

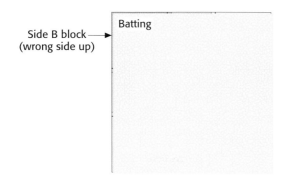

Side B block (wrong side up) → Batting

3. Referring to "Block Variation 2" on page 18, use the blue, yellow, and orange strips to make block 1. Refer to your colored sketch for correct color shading and be sure to keep the Nine Patch block from side B in its correct orientation.

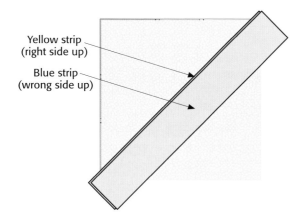

Yellow strip (right side up)
Blue strip (wrong side up)

4. Repeat to make blocks 4, 13, and 16.

5. Refer to "Block Variation 6" on page 19 and make 12 blocks, using the units made for side A. Refer to your sketch and keep all the Nine Patch blocks in the correct orientation.

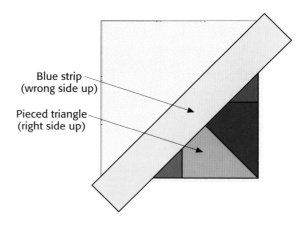

Blue strip (wrong side up)
Pieced triangle (right side up)

QUILT ASSEMBLY

1. Trim all the blocks to 9½" x 9½".

2. Refer to "Basic Sashing" on page 21 and "Pieced Sashing" on page 22 for details as needed. You will need to piece the 1⅛"-wide blue, yellow, and orange sashing strips for side A. Piece them with a diagonal seam, where necessary, and then cut to fit the block.

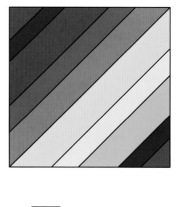

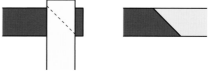

3. Join the blocks and rows with sashing strips.

4. Determine the arrangement of the border strips for side B of the quilt.

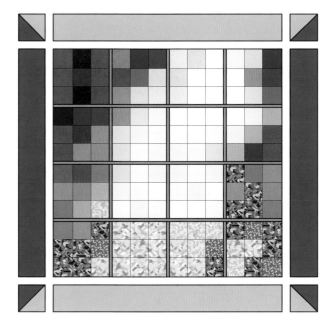

5. Layer a 5"-wide batting strip between two fabric border strips. Pin or spray-baste, and quilt as desired. Make four border strips. Trim the border strips to 4½" x the length and width of your quilt.

6. Place a 5" border square for side A, right side down, on your work surface and cover it with a 5" batting square. Referring to "Block Variation 1" on page 17, use the light and dark blue triangles to make four blocks. Trim each block to 4½" x 4½".

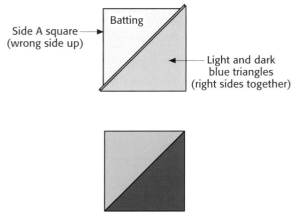

Make 4.

Note: To achieve the look of "attic windows" on side B, it was necessary to use corner squares, made with light and dark blue triangles, on the border. If one side of the border has corner squares, the other side must also, even though by using the same fabric the squares just disappear.

7. Referring to "Borders with Corner Squares" on page 24, join the side border pieces to the quilt with sashing strips. Join the corner squares to the ends of the remaining border pieces with sashing strips, making sure you place the triangle squares correctly. Join these to the quilt with sashing strips.

8. Using the pattern on page 93 and referring to the photo of side B on page 78, appliqué a cat on the "windowsill." I suggest that you hand appliqué it and go through the top layer only.

9. Referring to "Basic Binding" on page 26 or "Reversible Binding" on page 28, cut strips and bind the edges of the quilt. To maintain the illusion of depth achieved by using light and dark blue fabric in the borders on side B, bind them with the same fabrics.

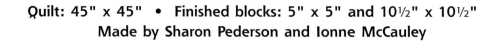

Quilt: 45" x 45" • Finished blocks: 5" x 5" and 10½" x 10½"
Made by Sharon Pederson and Ionne McCauley

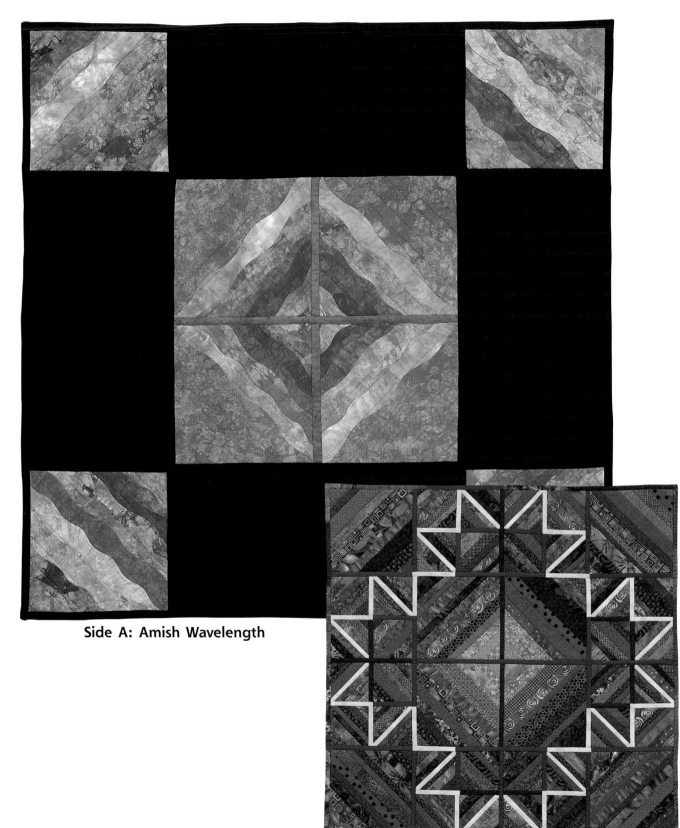

Side A: Amish Wavelength

Side B: Sashing in the Spotlight

ALTERED AMISH

*O*ne of the best things about working with a friend on any project is the way ideas just take off. Ionne and I were discussing how to incorporate the remaining ideas that we really wanted to include in the book. Our "must include" list had some things that didn't seem to fit into one quilt. That was while we were still thinking inside the box. Then, late one afternoon after we had quit for the day (OK, I'll admit we had had a relaxing glass of wine), we realized that the ideas we had would not only work well together, they would be fun to do.

Ionne wanted to make an Amish-style quilt; I wanted to make something with wavy lines, and I also wanted to make a quilt where the sashing created the interest. In short order we figured out that the three ideas could be included in the same quilt.

By using wavy strips on the Amish side, we took care of two of our design ideas. And, as we worked within the framework of the Amish hanging diamond, the quilt lent itself wonderfully to the idea I had of designing with sashing. This is another great example of two heads being better than one.

MATERIALS

Yardages are based on 42"-wide fabric.

Side A

- 1½ yards total of assorted hand-dyed fabrics for wavy strips
- 1⅛ yards of black for small blocks
- ¾ yard of black for 1¾"-wide sashing
- ½ yard of purple hand-dyed fabric for large blocks
- ¼ yard of blue for 1¾"-wide sashing

Side B

- 2 yards total of assorted navy blue prints and solids for blocks

- ⅜ yard of lime green fabric for 1⅛"-wide sashing strips and blocks
- ⅜ yard of blue fabric for 1⅛"-wide sashing strips

Basic Binding

- ½ yard

Reversible Binding

- ¼ yard for 1⅛"-wide strips
- ⅜ yard for 1¾"-wide strips

Batting and Supplies

- ¾ yard of 96"-wide fusible batting
- The WaveEdge Ruler (see "Resources" on page 94)

Cutting

From the batting, cut:

8 squares, 11½" x 11½"

32 squares, 6" x 6"

From the purple hand-dyed fabric, cut:

2 squares, 12½" x 12½"; cut once on the
diagonal to yield 4 triangles

From the black fabric for small blocks, cut:

32 squares, 6" x 6"

From the lime green fabric, cut:

8 strips, 1⅛" x 42"

**From the assorted navy blue prints and
solids, cut:**

Narrow, medium, and wide strips as needed

Side A

I strongly recommend making a practice block
with the WaveEdge Ruler before starting on
your project. The instructions with the ruler are
good, but I had to practice cutting strips and
then make a couple of blocks before I felt
completely comfortable with the technique.
There are no specific cutting instructions for the
wavy strips because you will vary them to suit
yourself.

1. With the fabric right side up, align the long
   edge of a purple triangle with a line on your
   cutting mat. Also right side up, place the first
   strip of hand-dyed fabric so that the left side
   overlaps the long edge of the triangle by 1".

2. Place the WaveEdge Ruler on top of the
   strips so that the right line on the ruler is on
   the left edge of the top piece of fabric. Use

the long, gentle-curve edge of the ruler. With
a small rotary cutter, cut through both pieces
of fabric. Remove the trimming.

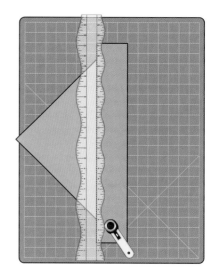

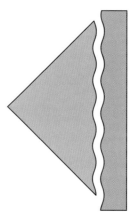

3. Turn the strip over so that the two curved
   edges are right sides together and match up
   the hills and valleys. Make four or five clips,
   about ¼" apart and ⅛" deep, into the valleys
   of both pieces.

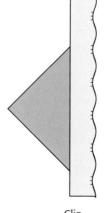

Clip.

4. Return the strip to its original position, with the hills and valley opposite each other; turn so that the right sides are together again and pin the middle of each hill to the middle of its valley.

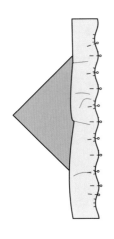

5. With a ¼" foot on your machine, place the beginning of the strip in your machine, making sure you have lined up the two ends. Anchor your stitches, gently bring the two edges together, and stitch. The edge of the triangle is bias so be very careful you do not stretch it.

6. Press the seam toward the strip. Line up the straight edge of the strip you have just sewn on your cutting mat and repeat with the next strip. Each successive strip will be shorter because you are sewing a triangle shape. Trim to 11½" x 11½". Make four.

Make 4.

7. Make four more blocks using strips cut with the WaveEdge Ruler, but this time with no triangle. Begin in the middle of the block and refer to "Block Variation 2" on page 18 as needed. Trim to 11½" x 11½".

8. Arrange the blocks on a design wall and number as in the diagram. You will have only 8 of the 16 blocks made at this point. The remaining 8 blocks are all black.

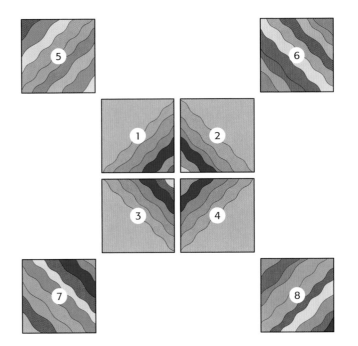

SIDE B

1. Layer a 6" black square with a 6" square of fusible batting. Fuse together. Make 32.

2. Using the 6" squares of batting with black and referring to "Block Variation 3" on page 18, make 16 blocks using lime green strips for the center strip and all other strips blue. Then referring to "Block Variation 2" on page 18, make 16 blocks using all blue strips. Trim to 5½" x 5½".

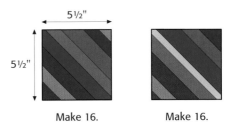

Make 16.   Make 16.

3. Working with one block at a time, fuse side A block 1 to an 11½" square of fusible batting. Referring to "Block Variation 2" on page 18, the photo of side B on page 84, and the quilt

diagram below, sew narrow, medium, and wide blue strips to the block, grading the color from dark to light. The light half should correspond to the wavy strips on the other side. Make sure you have the diagonal going the right way on each block. It should be going in the same direction as the side A block. Remember to use invisible thread in the bobbin. Trim to 11" x 11". Repeat with blocks 2, 3, and 4.

4. Repeat with side A blocks 5, 6, 7, and 8, using navy blue prints only. Again, be sure the strips are going in the same direction on both sides. Trim to 11" x 11".

QUILT ASSEMBLY

1. On a design wall, arrange the side B blocks as in the diagram. Make sure the larger blocks are in their correct numbered positions.

2. Refer to "Basic Sashing" on page 21 and "Pieced Sashing" on page 22. Sew the 5½" blocks and rows together with lime green or

navy blue sashing strips as shown in the diagram. All side A sashing will be black except for the four center squares.

Side B

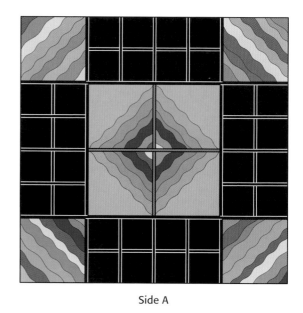

Side A

3. Referring to "Basic Binding" on page 26 or "Reversible Binding" on page 28, cut strips and bind the edges of the quilt.

NOT ENOUGH CATS

I must have suffered fabric deprivation in a previous lifetime, because I have been hoarding Japanese and African fabric for years. I would often take the fabrics out and fondle them, but I wouldn't dare use them! One night during a bout of insomnia, I had a talk with myself. I got up the next morning and pulled out all the previously hoarded African fabric and started cutting it up. Horrors! But the world did not come to an end, so I carried on.

I had a picture in my mind of an old string-pieced quilt set in long vertical strips with some of the string piecing strips going up and down and others going sideways. Another idea I wanted to explore was to "hide" the sashing by making it look like part of the block. The two ideas seemed to go together, so one side was planned.

Then I remembered a favorite quilt I made when I first learned to machine appliqué: cats appliquéd on a dark background. That was something I wanted to do again, but this time I vowed to use my hoarded Japanese fabrics. Thus, "Not Enough Cats" was born.

MATERIALS
Yardages are based on 42"-wide fabric.

Side A
- 1⅜ yards of navy blue fabric for background
- 1¼ yards total of assorted Japanese prints for cats
- ⅞ yard of Japanese print for borders

Side B
- 1½ yards total of assorted African prints
- 1½ yards total of assorted solid fabrics
- ⅞ yard of African print for borders*

2"-wide Sashing
- ¾ yard of navy blue print
- ¾ yard of black fabric

Basic Sashing
- ¼ yard for 1⅛"-wide strips
- ¼ yard for 1¾"-wide strips

Basic Binding
- ⅝ yard

Reversible Binding
- ⅜ yard for 1⅛"-wide strips
- ½ yard for 1¾"-wide strips

Batting
- 1⅛ yards of 96"-wide fusible batting

You will need extra fabric if you want to fussy cut.

Quilt: 44" x 62½" • Finished block: 9½" x 12¼"
Made by Ionne McCauley and Sharon Pederson

Side A: Japanese Cats

Side B: African Strings

CUTTING

From the batting, cut:

12 rectangles, 10½" x 13¼"

2 strips, 4½" x 35"

2 strips, 4½" x 65"

From the navy blue background fabric, cut:

12 rectangles, 10½" x 13¼"

From the assorted African prints and solid fabrics, cut:

Approximately 30 rectangles, 3" x 13¼"

Approximately 36 rectangles, 3" x 10½"

From the Japanese border print, cut:

5 strips, 4½" x 42"

From the African border print, cut:

5 strips, 4½" x 42"

SIDE A

1. Using the pattern on page 93 and your favorite appliqué method, cut out and appliqué cats onto the 10½" x 13¼" navy blue rectangles. Make 12 blocks.

Make 12.

Sharon's Suggestion

You can have some of your cats facing east and some facing west if you prefer. Remember to reverse the template if you choose to do that.

2. Arrange the cat blocks on a design wall. Leave them there until you are ready to fuse them to the side B blocks.

SIDE B

1. Cut the African-print and solid rectangles into wedges as shown. Vary the angle from piece to piece so the strips are random.

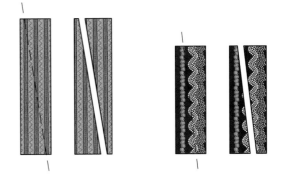

2. With the wide part at the bottom, place a 13¼" wedge-shaped piece of African fabric, right side up, onto a batting rectangle, matching the left raw edge of the fabric with the left raw edge of the batting. With the wide part at the top, place a solid 13¼" wedge piece, right sides together, on the African fabric, matching raw edges. Sew to the batting with a ¼" seam. Flip open and finger-press the seam.

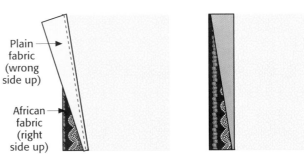

Plain fabric (wrong side up)

African fabric (right side up)

3. Alternating print and solid fabrics and alternating the wide part from bottom to top, continue sewing wedges onto the batting until it is covered. Fuse the strips to the batting by holding the iron ⅛" away. Make 6 blocks.

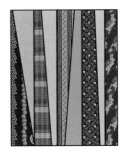

Make 6.

4. Repeat with the 10½" wedges and turn the batting the opposite direction. Make 6 blocks.

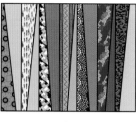

Make 6.

QUILT ASSEMBLY

1. Working with one block at a time, place a side A block (a cat) on the batting of a side B block (African fabric) and fuse. Follow the quilt diagram to be sure you have the correct orientation of the block on side B. You will be alternating a vertical and a horizontal block on side B.

2. With invisible thread in the bobbin, quilt in the ditch around the appliquéd cat.

3. Trim the block to 10" x 12¾" and return it to the design wall.

4. Repeat for all 12 blocks.

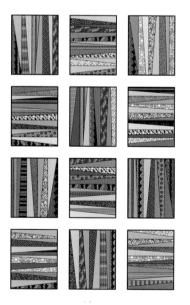

5. Referring to "Basic Sashing" on page 21, sew the blocks together. To blur the edges of the blocks on side B, use one of the African

fabrics for sashing rather than the black fabric that will be used for the wider sashing between the rows.

6. Cut 2½"-wide sashing strips from side A and side B sashing fabrics and referring to "Wide Sashing" on page 23, sew the rows together.

7. Join the five 4½" x 42" border strips for side A end to end to make one long strip. Cut two pieces 4½" x 35" for the top and bottom borders. Cut two pieces 4½" x 65" for the side borders. Repeat with side B border fabrics.

8. Layer a batting strip between the fabric border strips. Fuse and quilt as desired. Trim the length to match the measurements of your quilt.

9. Referring to "Borders with a Contrasting Inner Border" on page 25, join the top and bottom border strips to the quilt with contrasting sashing strips. Referring to "Pieced Sashing" on page 22, cut and sew a border fabric rectangle to each end of the sashing strips for the sides. Make two for each side of the quilt. Join the side borders to the quilt with the pieced sashing strips.

10. Referring to "Basic Binding" on page 26 or "Reversible Binding" on page 28, cut strips and bind the edges of the quilt.

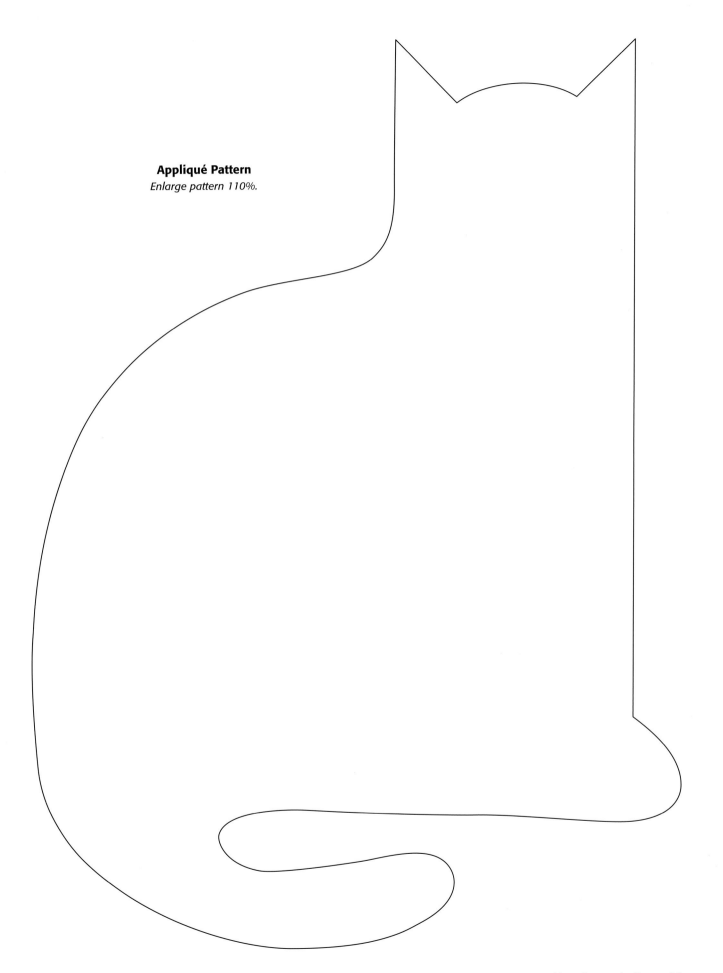

Appliqué Pattern
Enlarge pattern 110%.

RESOURCES

Indonesian Batiks
14816 Hoxie Lane
Anacortes, WA 98221
360-299-3968
www.indobatiks.com

The WaveEdge Ruler
www.thewaveedgeruler.com

The Binding Miter Tool
Jackie Robinson
Animas Quilts Publishing
830 Douglas Hill Road
Eureka, MT 59917
email: jackie@animas.com
www.animas.com

Quilter's BlockButler
1004 141st Place NE
Bellevue, WA 98007
www.blockbutler.com

OESD (Oklahoma Embroidery Supply & Design, Inc.)
12101 I-35 Service Road
Oklahoma City, OK 73131
405-359-2741
www.oesd.com
This is a wonderful source of machine embroidery designs you can download.

Ionne McCauley
ionmcc@nanaimo.ark.com
As well as being my "right-hand person" on this book, Ionne is a wonderful teacher who loves to do commission pieces. She also does custom hand-dyed fabrics. To see some of her work, visit the Gallery on my Web site at www.sharonquilts.com.

Mary Ellen Kranz
mekranz@prodigy.net
Mary Ellen teaches a killer class in computer skills for quilters and an equally wonderful class in how to manipulate photographs and print them onto fabric using your computer. She has a book (publication date October 2004) from The Electric Quilt Company called *Blending Photos with Fabric*.

Martingale & Company
20205 144th Avenue NE
Woodinville, WA 98072-8478
800-426-3126
www.martingale-pub.com
Photo-transfer paper; *Quilting Your Memories: Inspirations for Designing with Image Transfers* and *Quilting More Memories: Creating Projects with Image Transfers*, two books by Sandy Bonsib

Bernina
www.bernina.com
Sewing machines

Hobbs Bonded Fibers
www.hobbsbondedfibers.com
The makers of many fine battings including Hobbs Fusible Batting, which I use almost exclusively.

Printed Treasures
www.printedtreasures.com
The makers of treated fabric sheets that you can use in your inkjet printer.

ABOUT THE AUTHOR

Sharon Pederson was born and raised in Vancouver, British Columbia. She learned to sew from her mother when she was very young. In fact, Sharon was so young that she could not reach the treadle of the sewing machine while sitting on the seat. To sew, she would stand on one leg and treadle with the other. Her mother insists she had no choice in the matter; Sharon was determined to sew—right then!

Sharon married young and had two wonderful daughters, Gail and Heather. Then she grew up and divorced. For many years, she worked as a political organizer, traveling from coast to coast in Canada.

The year 1986 was a big one for Sharon—she remarried and discovered quilting. When she started to teach quilting, Sharon realized that she preferred the creative world of quilting to political organizing, so she gave up politics to become a full-time quilting teacher.

In 1996 Sharon was on the road again after she took a job as a sales rep for a wholesale fabric distributor. She also continued to teach and was hardly ever home. After four years of selling fabric to quilt shops, Sharon retired with a house full of swatches and returned to her first loves: making quilts and teaching.

When not traveling to teach, Sharon is living happily ever after in a small house filled with quilts and fabric; her wonderful, supportive husband; and a very neurotic cat.

You can visit Sharon at www.sharonquilts.com.

New and Bestselling Titles from

Martingale ®
& C O M P A N Y
America's Best-Loved Craft & Hobby Books®
America's Best-Loved Knitting Books®

That Patchwork Place®

America's Best-Loved Quilt Books®

NEW RELEASES
300 Paper-Pieced Quilt Blocks
American Doll Quilts
Classic Crocheted Vests
Dazzling Knits
Follow-the-Line Quilting Designs
Growing Up with Quilts
Hooked on Triangles
Knitting with Hand-Dyed Yarns
Lavish Lace
Layer by Layer
Lickety-Split Quilts
Magic of Quiltmaking, The
More Nickel Quilts
More Reversible Quilts
No-Sweat Flannel Quilts
One-of-a-Kind Quilt Labels
Patchwork Showcase
Pieced to Fit
Pillow Party!
Pursenalities
Quilter's Bounty
Quilting with My Sister
Seasonal Quilts Using Quick Bias
Two-Block Appliqué Quilts
Ultimate Knitted Tee, The
Vintage Workshop, The
WOW! Wool-on-Wool Folk Art Quilts

APPLIQUÉ
Appliquilt in the Cabin
Blossoms in Winter
Garden Party
Shadow Appliqué
Stitch and Split Appliqué
Sunbonnet Sue All through the Year

HOLIDAY QUILTS & CRAFTS
Christmas Cats and Dogs
Christmas Delights
Hocus Pocus!
Make Room for Christmas Quilts
Welcome to the North Pole

LEARNING TO QUILT
101 Fabulous Rotary-Cut Quilts
Happy Endings, Revised Edition
Loving Stitches, Revised Edition
More Fat Quarter Quilts
Quilter's Quick Reference Guide, The
Sensational Settings, Revised Edition
Simple Joys of Quilting, The
Your First Quilt Book (or it should be!)

PAPER PIECING
40 Bright and Bold Paper-Pieced Blocks
50 Fabulous Paper-Pieced Stars
Down in the Valley
Easy Machine Paper Piecing
For the Birds
Papers for Foundation Piecing
Quilter's Ark, A
Show Me How to Paper Piece
Traditional Quilts to Paper Piece

QUILTS FOR BABIES & CHILDREN
Easy Paper-Pieced Baby Quilts
Easy Paper-Pieced Miniatures
Even More Quilts for Baby
More Quilts for Baby
Quilts for Baby
Sweet and Simple Baby Quilts

ROTARY CUTTING/SPEED PIECING
365 Quilt Blocks a Year Perpetual
    Calendar
1000 Great Quilt Blocks
Burgoyne Surrounded
Clever Quarters
Clever Quilts Encore
Endless Stars
Once More around the Block
Pairing Up
Stack a New Deck
Star-Studded Quilts
Strips and Strings
Triangle-Free Quilts

SCRAP QUILTS
Easy Stash Quilts
Nickel Quilts
Rich Traditions
Scrap Frenzy
Successful Scrap Quilts

TOPICS IN QUILTMAKING
Asian Elegance
Batiks and Beyond
Bed and Breakfast Quilts
Coffee-Time Quilts
Dutch Treat
English Cottage Quilts
Fast-Forward Your Quilting
Machine-Embroidered Quilts
Mad about Plaid!
Romantic Quilts
Simple Blessings

CRAFTS
20 Decorated Baskets
Beaded Elegance
Blissful Bath, The
Collage Cards
Creating with Paint
Holidays at Home
Pretty and Posh
Purely Primitive
Stamp in Color
Trashformations
Warm Up to Wool
Year of Cats…in Hats!, A

KNITTING & CROCHET
365 Knitting Stitches a Year Perpetual
    Calendar
Beyond Wool
Classic Knitted Vests
Crocheted Aran Sweaters
Crocheted Lace
Crocheted Socks!
Garden Stroll, A
Knit it Now!
Knits for Children and Their Teddies
Knits from the Heart
Knitted Throws and More
Knitter's Template, A
Little Box of Scarves, The
Little Box of Sweaters, The
Style at Large
Today's Crochet
Too Cute! Cotton Knits for Toddlers

Our books are available at
bookstores and your favorite
craft, fabric, and yarn retailers.
If you don't see the title
you're looking for, visit us at
www.martingale-pub.com
or contact us at:

1-800-426-3126

International: 1-425-483-3313
Fax: 1-425-486-7596
Email: info@martingale-pub.com

6/04